# Insight and Interpretation

# Insight and Interpretation

## The Essential Tools
of Psychoanalysis

### Roy Schafer

OTHER
Other Press
*New York*

The author gratefully acknowledges the following publishers for their kind permission to reprint as chapters of this book the articles listed below:

Chapter 4 was originally published in *The International Journal of Psycho-Analysis*, vol. 78, under the title "Vicissitudes of Remembering in the Countertransference." Copyright by The Institute of Psycho-Analysis, London, 1997.

Chapter 6 was originally published in *Psychoanalytic Psychology*, vol. 46. Copyright by The American Psychological Association, Washington, DC, 1999.

Chapter 7 was originally published in *The Annual of Psychoanalysis*, vol. 30, under the title "On Male Nonnormative Sexuality and Perversion in Psychoanalytic Discourse." Copyright by The Analytic Press, Hillsdale, NJ, 2002.

Chapter 8 was originally published in *Studies in Gender and Sexuality*, vol. 2. Copyright by The Analytic Press, Hillsdale, NJ, 2001.

Copyright © 2003 Roy Schafer

Production Editor: Robert D. Hack

This book was set in 11 pt. Goudy by Alpha Graphics of Pittsfield, NH.

10  9  8  7  6  5  4  3  2  1

**Library of Congress Cataloging-in-Publication Data**
Schafer, Roy.
    Insight and interpretation : the essential tools of psychoanalysis /
Roy Schafer.
        p. cm.
    Includes bibliographical references and index.
    ISBN 1-59051-047-X (alk. paper)
    1. Psychoanalysis.   2. Sex (Psychology)   3. Psychotherapy–Philosophy.
4. Freud, Sigmund, 1856–1939.   I. Title.
BF173 .S3277 2003
150.19'5–dc21
                                                                2003007776

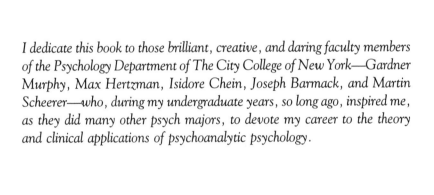

*I dedicate this book to those brilliant, creative, and daring faculty members of the Psychology Department of The City College of New York—Gardner Murphy, Max Hertzman, Isidore Chein, Joseph Barmack, and Martin Scheerer—who, during my undergraduate years, so long ago, inspired me, as they did many other psych majors, to devote my career to the theory and clinical applications of psychoanalytic psychology.*

# Contents

# Acknowledgments

Once again, I thank particularly my wife, Dr. Rita V. Frankiel, and my friend and colleague, Dr. William I. Grossman, for their continuing generous encouragement and their critical suggestions; they have been an invaluable source of help in getting on with the work reported here. I also acknowledge the steady assistance of Victoria Wright in preparing the manuscript copy and the consistently helpful role of my editors at Other Press, Stacy Hague and Bob Hack.

Again, a special thanks to Lanileigh Ting for her help.

# Preface

I regard this book as a continuation of my efforts to supplement the invaluable contributions to the lives of human beings initiated by Freud and carried forward by generations of dedicated psychoanalysts after him, and I submit it to my readers with the hope that their participation in this tradition will benefit from my further reflections, proposals, and reports of clinical work.

The essays that follow cluster around what I consider to be the central themes of my writings on clinical, theoretical, and applied psychoanalysis: insight and interpretation. No aspect of insight and interpretation is given. Analytic material is complex, and inferences from it are often uncertain. Psychoanalysis is a process of construing meaning and constructing influential ways of telling it to others. In the instance of analysands, these are others who are ambivalent both about being understood in ways that makes them conscious of what they have repudiated and about acting on this understanding to undertake change. In each case, analysts learn as they go along what each analysand can hear and use creatively for adaptive purposes. Analysts are also obligated to do what they can to meet the standard of accomplishing their task impartially, that is, in a manner that is not dominated by their own conflicts and values but rather regulated by the systematic analytic approach to which they have committed themselves and the meanings that that approach leads them to infer and interpret.

Therefore, considered in its entirety, clinical analytic listening is not what might be called natural or commonsense listening, though it does partake of that, too. No form of listening warrants the simple designation natural, for while it might seem and feel entirely atheoretical and based on self-evident truths, it is never free from the influence of unformulated methods of making sense, each with theoretical implications of its own and all of it dominated by a jumble of preconceptions and values. Put a number of "natural" listeners together, and each of them will hear things in a more or less different way. In court, apparently unbiased witnesses don't tell the same story.

In Part I, "Insights and Its Vicissitudes," I take up conceptual and technical problems that analysts encounter as they try to understand and communicate with their analysands and colleagues; these problems center on how to select, organize, retain, recall, and retell their analytic understanding of the material on which they have been working. Many colleagues with whom the analyst is communicating are likely to be more or less differently oriented theoretically or, even within the same school of thought, somewhat differently oriented clinically, and so they are likely to respond ambivalently, if not dismissively, to the insights being formulated. For example, in recent years much controversy has developed over the question of how to conceptualize the interaction of the two participants in the analytic process. It is now generally agreed that, inevitably, personal factors influence the analyst's point of view on what is encountered or evoked as well as what *should be* encountered or evoked, such as certain specific manifestations of sex and aggression in the transference. However, many of the propositions concerning countertransference and intersubjectivity that have been put forward in this connection have been based on incompatible theoretical systems and technical approaches. Among other things, these variations feature somewhat different ideas of objectivity, evidence, and truth. As a result, the possibility of productive debate is severely limited. Therefore, it should occasion no surprise that, as yet, no consensus has been reached. Debate continues as to the nature, extent, and weight to be given to the influence that personal issues specific to the analyst exert on the analytic process. Also continuously debated is how best to deal with that influence, a case in point being arguments that are advanced in favor of the analyst's more or less selectively disclosing personal feelings about the analysand to him or her.

Owing to the great influence of differing presuppositions about the human mind and human relationships, it is unlikely that a consensus will ever be reached on issues of technique. I will note these theoretical and clinical controversies throughout this book. I will devote special attention to some of them in Chapter 5, "Intimate Neutrality," and, taking them as a group, I have had them constantly in mind in developing my concluding chapter, "Knowing Another Person Psychoanalytically."

It must also be emphasized here that excellent critical reviews of hermeneutic and narrational aspects of insight and interpretation have appeared in the last decade, notably those by Strenger (1991), Lamm (1993), and Saks (1999). Although these authors, particularly Strenger and Saks, recognize the merits of the hermeneutic and narratological perspectives on psychoanalysis, they also advance arguments as to their limits and point out what they regard as other difficulties in hermeneutic presentations. It would take an extended book-review essay to rehearse and sort out these critiques, some of which take issue with my views. To undertake that project would, I believe, detract from my present effort to state and apply my position as concisely and persuasively as possible. The interested reader would do well to consult these sources. Lamm's work, unfortunately, has not received the critical attention it deserves. Its analysis of how we think about the past is especially to be recommended.

In Part II, "Applications," I present three essays dealing with insight and interpretation in the realm of sexuality. Each chapter comes at sexuality differently. The first concerns clinical work directly; the second—on non-normative male sexuality and perversion—extends into the linguistic and psychosocial realms, and so does the third which deals with jokes that, upon interpretation, can be seen to be as much about sexual politics as about the various aspects of intimate sexual relationships and feelings. I entitled Part II "Applications" to contrast it to Part I, in which the primary focus is on the basic premises and clinical operations required to develop psychoanalytic insights and interpretations.

Part III, "An Overview," pulls together all that has come before, and to some extent expands on it. However, it is not so much a summary as a relatively formal, systematic presentation of my essential ideas about insight and interpretation. In it I both state as best I can the methodological and epistemological constraints emphasized throughout the text, and try to work consistently within these constraints. Much in evidence will be my previously published critiques and proposals for modification or change of basic concepts and—not at all radically—for technical adjustments to these proposals. Particularly prominent in this regard are my forays into the theories of internalization (1968), action (1976), the analytic attitude (1983), narration and dialogue (1992), and, most recently, my simultaneous use of neo-Kleinian approach to doing analysis and the mid-twentieth century ego psychological clarifications and extensions of Freud's metapsychology proposed particularly by Hartmann, Kris, and Loewenstein (1997a, 1997b). Thus, in its theoretical aspect, the book deals with reconceptualizations, new conceptualization, and confrontations with pluralism, relativism, authority, objectivity, and some new perspectives on technique, whereas in its strictly technical aspects it explores further implications of traditional Freudian-Kleinian practices.

I consider it a necessary part of developing a point of view on insight and interpretation to scrutinize the uses of these concepts in a variety of contexts. Repeating, reviewing, and reworking psychoanalytic propositions in this way is as necessary as taking similar steps in clinical working through. Consequently, the reader will encounter some duplication of content and more than one review of familiar ideas and practices. It should also be noted that, in the interest of coherence and continuity, I have changed some stylistic and organizational features of previously published material and added and subtracted bits here and there, always taking care that these revisions not substantially change any of my arguments.

Although the three parts of the book were never intended to cover the whole of psychoanalysis—and certainly they do not do so—they do indicate the impressive scope and complexity of the problems that analysts face and the demands they must meet to function in the responsible, empathic, subtle, and patient way that distinguishes effective psychoanalytic work.

# PART I

---

## Insight and Its Vicissitudes

# Introduction to Part I

From the first, *insight* has occupied so central a place in psycho-analytic discourse that it has seemed the very essence of psychoanalysis, both clinical and applied. Clinically, it has been used regularly to refer to analysands integrating into their functioning the content of the interpretations formulated and proposed by their analysts. Further, it has been recognized that the analyst does not work alone. As the process moves along, analysands become better prepared and consciously more willing to collaborate in developing analytically informed and sound interpretations, even if, owing to their conflicts, they do not do so consistently.

In the first three chapters—"Insight into Insight," "Insight for Whom?" and "Insight: Seeing or Telling?"—the idea of insight will be considered conceptually and technically. Each essay should at least clarify significant aspects of what we mean by psychoanalytic insight. The technical issues to be addressed include deciding what requires interpretation, enhancing analysands' readiness to work toward insight, and facilitating their sense of mastery of important and personally characteristic tendencies hitherto unrecognized because they have been repudiated and therefore repressed, projected, or otherwise defended against.

Following this exploration of the implications and entailments of insight and its uses in interpretation, I will consider some special problems associated with keeping track of the analytic process as it moves along, for it is always necessary to remain alert to influences stemming from both the nature of the analytic interaction and the analyst's personality make-up. Combined, these influences can disrupt accurate and timely remembering of what has already transpired. Even in the ongoing session, it can at times be hard to keep track of who said what to whom. Insight and interpretation are bound to suffer when these influences go unnoticed or unattended.

Then, in the concluding chapter of Part I, I will take up directly a topic that has entered the preceding chapters at various points: the analyst's neutrality, that is, his or her relatively balanced, impartial approach to all aspects of the analysand's conflicts and maladaptive patterns of living. The large question to be faced here—it is one that is at the center of much current controversy—is the extent to which claims of neutrality can be sustained in the face of all the insights that have been gained into the mutually stimulating aspects of the analytic dialogue and the personal factors that go into the making of the psychoanalyst.

To prepare the stage for these chapters, I will first present a brief summary of what I take to be some widely held, existing ideas about insight, its attainment, and its consequences. I consider this preparatory move necessary not to clear away these familiar views as though they are obstructive mistakes—mostly, they are not—but to indicate the baseline with reference to which I will be presenting my slant on the many issues that I believe require further clarification, exploration, and modification.

## BASELINE: PSYCHOANALYTIC INSIGHT AS COMMONLY UNDERSTOOD

Usually, the contents of influential interpretations are arrived at through analysis of transference, defense, and (now more than ever) countertransference. However, the development of that content may begin with analysis of material external to the analytic situation, such as problems at work or experiences in the family. These crucial interpretations define unconscious fantasies and conflicting tendencies ascribable to the three major psychic structures—id, ego, and superego—and their mutual accommodating, oppositional, and compromising relations. At the center of this material are two central and inevitably interrelated sources of material, one the unconscious fantasies that are developed around intense and changing bodily experience, and the other, unconscious fantasies about real or imagined relations with others who have figured significantly in the analysand's development or are now playing active roles in her or his daily life. To the extent that the childhood roots of fantasy and conflict are clear enough and timely to mention, interpretations sometimes extend to them as well. Doing so in an unintellectualized, rounded, and timely way facilitates further development and integration of many partial insights.

In general, analytic insight has been understood to refer to the analysand's rational, conscious and preconscious grasp and modification of the unconscious issues that, preanalytically, have been lived out in blind repetitions (Freud 1917). Adaptive grasp and mastery of this hitherto split-off material enables the analysand to deal more realistically, creatively, and therefore effectively with the difficulties and conflicts that inevitably arise simply from one's being in the world and that have now been transferred to being in analysis.

In this traditional account, achieving insight tends to take on a somewhat rationalist coloring. The rationalist emphasis becomes evident in discussions that feature frequent use of phrases that convey the idea of gaining understanding, seeing the light, grasping what something *really* means, finding the cause, and getting the right answer. This is so even if, simultaneously, it is being emphasized that the idea of insight is not free of ambiguity and the route to apparent insight is often painfully rocky (exacerbated anxiety, guilt, shame, depression, and so on); also, that one cannot always count on analysands' convinced acceptance and use of their new insight. For the difficulty of access to insight, particularly in the context of the transference relationship, testifies to the dread the analysands unavoidably experience and must work through before making it their own and beginning to live differently and, in their terms, better. Intellectualized discussions of insight marginalize rather than center on the arduous work entailed by changing one's life insightfully.

Currently, many analysts are emphasizing the "real" relationship between analyst and analysand. They claim that it plays a major role in fostering beneficial change. The analytic process, they say, depends on much more than cognitive access to present versions of old and painful content, that is, insight and interpretation. Nevertheless, these same analysts continue to rely on insight and interpretation; for them, too, insight into unconscious content remains important in bringing about analytic change. Consequently, the following discussions are relevant to their work, too.

# 1

# Insight into Insight

The landmark contribution by Betty Joseph, "On Understanding and Not Understanding" (1983), explained and illustrated the value of the analyst's paying close attention to the meanings that analysands unconsciously ascribe to insight: both their fantasies about the insightful analyst's position in the clinical relationship and their fantasies about what they are letting themselves in for in that relationship and in their daily lives by possessing insight. For example, owning insight might imply having to give up one's rights to babyhood in the transference; alternatively, it might mean having become either omnipotent or dangerously dependent on the "knowing" analyst. Similarly, if the analysand experiences the analyst's attainment of understanding, however brilliant and convincing it might be, as an exciting and frightening, implicitly sexual invasion or as a moralistic condemnation, and if the analyst does not note and then undertake analysis of this experience, the interpretation's potential beneficial effects can be nullified, limited, or even needlessly painful and extremely disruptive. Psychoanalytic understanding can also threaten to introduce turmoil into relations with others.

Ostensibly, analysands have accepted the idea that the analytic process is aimed at developing the kind of understanding that will alleviate the distress for which treatment has been sought. Invariably, however, it emerges that, unconsciously, they are ambivalent about being in analysis: mistrustful; humiliated; fearing dependence; turned away from what are felt to be their own intolerable impulses, desires, states of mind, and moral, physical, intellectual, and social shortcomings; all this plus further opposition to change based on their being unconsciously attached to certain aspects of the very suffering from which, consciously, they desire relief and to the "bad objects" who, in their internal worlds, play an essential part in bringing on this suffering. For all these reasons and many others, analysands will view insight for a long time as, at best, a mixed blessing. They cannot be expected to collaborate in the work of analysis wholeheartedly; superficially, however, they may quickly become enthusiasts.

Matters can be made more complicated by analysts' fantasies about their work. The influence of these fantasies varies from one analyst to the next; it will be greater at some moments than others, stronger with some analysands than others, and in play more often with respect to certain kinds of content than others. However, and despite the growing clamor of claims to the contrary, it has not been demonstrated that the competent analyst's usual functioning is so dominated by these fantasies and the feelings they express that she or he is little more than a co-patient (see Chapter 5 on intimate neutrality). This is not to deny that it is always a good idea for analysts to do some self-analysis upon experiencing any heightened emotion while at work, especially when a self-righteous attitude is part of that reaction, and to scan their analysands' material for signs that this heightened emotionality has been influencing an analysand in a way that is throwing the analysis off course. For example, and like the analysand, the analyst might experience the pursuit and imparting of certain insights as voyeuristic, sadistic, rapacious, seductive, condescending, rejecting, or some combination of these and other troubling and often exciting tendencies. Upon analysis, many analysts' inhibitions in their work do seem to stem from defenses against their own disturbing and excited fantasies.

It is, however, equally important to note that the analyst might begin to view the work in one or more of these ways in response to the analysand's projective identifications. In these instances, projective influences may have stimulated residual but ordinarily subdued conflictual inclinations that have played a part in the analyst's choice of a career in the field of mental treatment (A. Reich 1951) or are peculiarly relevant to work with a certain analysand (Brenman Pick 1995). For example, identification with the analysand based on similar family experiences of abuse increases the analyst's susceptibility to the analysand's projective identifications concerning mistreatment. Long ago, Money-Kyrle (1958) pointed out that, in part, the analyst is always analyzing her or his child self, now projected into the analysand and both enhancing empathic understanding and opening up dangers of projective distortion. To this it may be added that other internal objects— parents, siblings, and so on—may also be projected into the analysand. Thus, putting the point most generally, projective identifications move in two directions, and it is often the case that projective identifications are empowered by both participants in the analytic process.

With all these subjective factors influencing the development and acceptance of understanding, we might restate Joseph's (1983) thesis: *developing insight into insight is an indispensable aspect of an effective analytic process.* Like all other insight, developing this extension of the work into the meanings and consequences of insight *for both participants* is a never-ending process, for the meaning of insight becomes ever more complex and reorganized as the analysis progresses.

It is safe to say, therefore, that one can never settle on a fixed, comprehensive, and definitive formulation of what insight means to the analysand and to the analyst, too, neither during nor after analysis. This is one of the inferences to be drawn from Freud's having characterized analysis as "interminable" (1937). Put otherwise, the development of insight is always taking place in the middle of things; we cannot know once and for all where insight begins, where it ends, and what it includes. Thus, we can never be done with it altogether.

A brief clinical example: In the midst of analysis, I pointed out to a male analysand, Max, that he was describing a disagreement with his wife so defensively that it seemed he was afraid he would give me the impression that he was being mean to her. He responded to this intervention as though I was advocating that he treat his wife more aggressively, and he reacted by clamming up. In this way he shifted the focus of interpretation away from his initial defensiveness in the transference to his newly defensive fantasy of me as a dangerously critical judge taking sides in the marital dispute. Max was not consciously receiving the interpretive comment as a potential move toward insight. I decided that at that time it would not have been helpful to the analysis—though I was tempted—to interpret his splitting and projecting into me his own wish to be more openly critical of his wife. It would have been premature to offer that interpretation because he would then have had to confront tendencies that he was not yet ready to recognize as his own. What was needed was my helping him focus both on his fantasy of my emotional position in the relationship and on how this fantasy left him feeling on the defensive then and there. Additionally, it is quite likely that by struggling with his account of his dealings with his wife, important as it was in its own right, he was already using her to displace comparable issues from the transference. Displacement helped Max keep the peace between us. The least helpful thing to have done in this kind of situation would have been to offer immediate, clarifying restatement and reassuring explanation of my neutral attitude.

Other analysands might put other constructions on the kind of analytic comments on marital conflict that I made in this case. For example, they might not hear my intervention as encouragement to act a certain way. Instead, they might hear it as criticism intended to expose their inherent meanness. If the interventions are so ill-timed that they are experienced as offensive, the analyst must consider the possibility that negative countertransference has played a role in this development.

Consider in this regard the status of insight once termination is in the air. The analysand might begin to regard prior development of beneficial understanding as a possible means of escape from analysis as from a prison. Alternatively, that development might be regarded as a basis for being rejected and abandoned by the analyst, as being reassured against some persisting feelings of failure, as a rite of passage to rebirth, or as a prelude to one's being replaced by the analyst's next "baby" or "lover." The result of an analyst's missing an analysand's construal of termination in any of these ways is likely to be unnecessarily awkward and disappointing analytic experiences of termination for both participants, most of all, of course, for the analysand.

In other instances the issue might be defense against good feelings, compliance, evasion, envy, intellectualization, or competitiveness. Although each of these issues is, of course, significant and deserves analytic attention in its own right, the analysand's dwelling on it ought not distract the analyst from what is being conveyed between the lines about insight itself, and through that about how the analytic relationship is being experienced. Technically, the problem remains essentially the same: how to understand the way the analysand construes the analyst's intervention and her or his intentions, possibly perceptively, and how to convey that insight to the analysand in a useful way.

John Steiner (1993) has referred to the type of intervention I am recommending as *analyst-centered interpretation*, that is, interpretation focused on how the analysand envisages the analyst's intentions in the relationship and the meaning the analyst intends to convey when interpreting. This interpretive shift to the analyst's psyche often helps open up difficult issues in transferences heavily burdened with persecutory fantasies. These transferences are not rare, so many analysands are burdened in just this way owing to their readiness to project their numerous and painful unconscious self-accusations. Analyst-centered interpretations are particularly helpful in promoting insight into insight.

Often, the content itself proves to contain cues as to what is going on in the insight-oriented relationship. For example, one analysand talked tonelessly about withdrawal from past relationships while evidently withdrawing emotionally from the analyst. In another instance, an analysand talked about losses in a flat, withdrawn way without mentioning the analyst's impending vacation. Not to be ignored is the possibility that the soon-to-depart analyst might already be showing subtle signs of being somewhat less available than usual in the sessions—withdrawn, to put it bluntly. Needless to say, there are many devices available to the analysand to try to seduce the analyst into actual or imagined blindness or into some other enactment that leads the dialogue away from currently heightened conflict. If the analyst consistently lets manifest content dominate her or his thoughts and neglects implied unconscious fantasies about the process of developing insight, enactment is likely to become a prominent part of the analytic scene.

Frequently, however, many missed opportunities may result from the analyst's having to switch rapidly from content to process and back again, while also keeping track of the often subtle continuity between content and process; all this at the same time as the analysand continues to switch focus or act out the very issues being discussed. For example, the analyst makes a point about a female analysand's tendency to play dumb because she hopes to induce an enactment of being scorned by the analyst, as she believes she had been in her family, and she then misses the point of his intervention and hears a "disgusted" analyst actually calling her stupid. In these situations, analysts cannot always keep up with their analysands, let alone stay one step ahead of them. It is not helpful to regard the actual or imagined enactments that ensue as mistakes. It is more useful and not at all self-deceptive to regard them as further material to be interpreted; for these "mistakes" are likely to be successful instances of the analysand's repetitive recreation of chronic problems in living with themselves and among people. It is unrealistic for the analyst to expect otherwise. Freud (1917) made it plain that these enactments point to the necessity of interpreting acting out as a substitute for direct emotional experience, remembering, and understanding.

## TWO SIGNIFICANT CONTRIBUTORS

In his studies of mental functioning and insight, Kris (see 1950, 1951, 1956a, b especially) takes up many issues that pertain to insight into insight, so that the present discussion could be considered further elaboration of some of his principal points. That Kris did not go further in these papers may be attributed to his keeping a steady focus on general metapsychological propositions concerning structure, function, psychic energy, and broad dynamics, all this in keeping with his project of refining and extending Freud's structural theory (ego psychology, so called). Only in his case examples does he show his perceptiveness with regard to unconscious transference fantasy; but within ego psychology, there had not been developed a means to integrate meaning, expressed in unconscious fantasy. In my present view, metapsychology, being a formalistic project superimposed on clinical work, is not designed to accommodate meaning, so that it is obviously inappropriate to attempt that development outside of a consistently clinical discourse.

Abrams (1996), the second contributor, has recommended a clinical approach that has many features in common with what has been presented here. However, his principal emphasis falls on *discovery* while mine falls on *construction*. Otherwise put, his approach is that of scientific realism while mine is hermeneutic and narratologically oriented. Additionally, his excellent case example suffers, in my opinion, from his seeming so set on adhering to joint egalitarian discovery that he does not take up the fantasies his female patient finally developed about what he intended to offer and the ways in which he was implementing it. It is as though Abrams' curiosity stopped short at the point where the patient rejected his approach, this despite Abrams' earlier recognition that there can be a great discrepancy between what is offered by the analyst and what is received by the analysand and his insight into the patient's experience of his approach at the onset of their work together. I suspect that these two differences between Abrams and me would be felt in the clinical situation and could influence the course of analysis, though I have no basis for claiming that in this particular case his patient's flight from analysis could have been averted. The value of Abrams' contribution lies in its showing how much more insight one can hope to develop when the analyst maintains the general analytic attitude on which both of us seem to agree.

## CONCLUDING REMARKS

Because analyst-centered interpretation keeps the analysis focused on fantasized versions of the analyst's interpretations and their emotional contexts, it promotes insight into insight—if anything can promote insight at moments of frightened alienation. Analyst-centered interpretation works this way by helping develop reflection on the process at a safe distance from the threatened self; one focuses on the analysand's experience of what the two participants are doing, whether collaboratively or in fantasized and unfortunately, sometimes actual antagonism. There is hardly a more effective way to bring forth and analyze transference, thereby promoting insight where it counts the most.

# 2

# Insight for Whom?

Traditionally, insight has been discussed as that which is to be imparted to analysands. It is they who are in need of insight. Without insight their lives will be cursed with blind repetitions of their painful pasts. In this account, the analyst's role is to develop insight *for them* through interpretation. The analyst is the vehicle of understanding and, of course, the facilitator of those changes that will enable analysands to grasp and use insight adaptively. Facilitating those changes, especially through analysis of defense, itself a work of insight, is an essential part of this process.

I believe that this traditional belief that insight is *for the analysand* is inexact. Insight must, of course, be *imparted to analysands*. Without insight, they cannot reorganize their visions of internal and external realities in ways that facilitate adaptation (Schafer 1970). And yet there is a sense in which it is correct and useful to maintain that, *primarily, insight is for the analyst*. How is this so? The answer comes in several parts.

First, it is usually the analyst who maintains a reasonably firm grasp on the insights that have been developed and on their potential usefulness in interventions that facilitate understanding and adaptation. Although analysts might modify, even reject, certain insights as the work progresses, they usually make these changes knowingly and deliberately, for they will have been maintaining the insights not as certainties but only as provisional formulations, much like hypotheses to be continuously reassessed in the light of further evidence. They regard insights as *true for the time being*. Only in some instances do they retain them unmodified. Attaining insight is an unending process.

For analysands, the case is usually quite different. Typically, they do not maintain insights stably and, in self-contradiction, they do not regard them as work-in-process and therefore provisional. Their insights are likely to be both highly unstable and concretely experienced. They can be quickly forgotten, reversed, transformed into harsh judgment, approval, command, gift, or enticement. Although they can change rapidly they also tend to be installed as truths that are difficult to question. Additionally, as Hartmann (1951, in 1964, p. 153) pointed out in his remarks on "multiple appeal" of interpretations, analysands often apply insights in other realms of conflict than those singled out by the analyst. Thus, there may be great distance between what the analyst intends and what the analysand does with what is proffered. Once formulated and communicated, the insights undergo continuing transformations. They are no longer under the analyst's control.

A second reason to revise our understanding of whom insight is for can be derived from the preceding considerations. It takes shape in what I have found to be a highly useful set of technical practices. As a set of recommendations they may seem so elementary they do not belong in this discussion; however, my observations while supervising and reflecting on other presentations lead me to believe that it is not as consistently remembered and put to use as I believe it should be. The point is this: analysts can facilitate further understanding by framing interventions in a manner that indicates that they are earnestly trying to understand what their analysands are conveying, and that this is so through all the verbal and nonverbal channels open to them in the analytic situation. In this way, analysts show that they view their role neither as one devoted to *explaining the analysand to himself or herself*, nor as one dedicated to *inducing what, unilaterally, they have decided is change for the better*. How in the world could one ever justify adopting that omniscient and controlling stance? For a long time, possibly forever, the analyst is not yet in a position to know what is "better" in each instance, and anyway he or she must rely on much future input from the analysand before beginning to identify *possible* benefits of the work and *conceivable* routes toward that betterment. New insight can add problems. Many surprises always lie ahead.

The purely explanatory stance—telling the analysand what's what and what's right to do—is deleterious to beneficial change of any depth not only because it is presumptuous, but also because it contributes greatly to the analysand's sense of being under pressure to submit to an omniscient and authoritarian analyst. Ultimately, that conception of the relationship leads to disillusionment and loss of faith in the analyst as a relatively secure figure, thereby severely limiting the analysis of transference. The most favorable atmosphere for analytic work is that of *searching* and thereby *facilitating* the analysand's readiness to search collaboratively; it is not that of *instructing* or triumphant *finding*.

To give a few examples of what is here suggested to be the more helpful way of communicating understanding: "Now I understand what you mean when you say that you can't talk about it; you expect me to be disgusted with you"; "So that for you it was a grueling experience because you felt so oppressed"; "What I gather from what you've been bringing out is that you are dissatisfied with the way things are going between us"; "So that's why you fell silent when you felt that wave of tenderness and concern; you thought I would brush it off"; "What your dream and the thoughts and feelings it stimulates suggest to me is that you were troubled by a sense of estrangement from me yesterday"; and "I don't yet understand where you are going with this." Much depends, of course, on timing and tone of voice and other vocal and postural dynamics, but what counts above all is the implied searching and facilitating attitude of the intervening analyst.

*Searching does not imply asking direct questions and expecting direct, analytically useful answers.* Direct questions can disrupt the flow of the session by pressing the analysand to shift level of abstraction or take distance from the tensions of the moment. This, too, can shake confidence in the analyst. Questions also encourage the idea that conscious thought alone, apart from instances in which an obscure detail requires clarification, can be counted on to increase analytic understanding. Because asking many questions discourages reliance on free association while limiting encounters with defenses against associating and getting to understand the need for these defenses, it inevitably makes the work superficial. For example, the directive questions, "What does that *remind* you of?" or "What do *you* make of that?" can compromise the attitude fostered by the less structuring question, "What comes to mind?" or by the analyst's just going on listening without showing a need to understand and respond to every bit of analytic movement. In the end, it is the larger drift, not the detail, which counts.

The analyst who works this way is not abandoning any claim to expertise. For these systematic interventions that convey what has been inferred or has remained obscure, though they are expressed in ordinary and provisional language and tone, are based on analytic sophistication. As such, they are more than likely to foster deeper understanding of the analysand's narrative and retain their potential to facilitate insightful change.

Also, it is usually helpful to formulate these facilitating interventions in the first person singular indicative: "I think"; "I suggest"; "The way I make sense of it is . . . "; and so on. Usually, speaking that way unostentatiously invites dialogue rather than submission or outright rejection. One wants to avoid *talking at* or *down to* the analysand as someone to be instructed and changed in predetermined ways. Optimally, the analyst *talks to* the analysand as someone with whom one is in a respectful, consequential, multidimensional conversation designed to increase mutual understanding, awareness of opportunities for change, and freedom to use these opportunities.

None of these suggestions are intended to avoid the analysand's defensive and transferential distortions of the analyst's interpretations. That hope betrays a serious misunderstanding of psycho-analytic principles. These principles prepare analysts to observe that and how analysands repetitively attempt to have their mal-adaptive way with whatever takes place during their sessions. If, for example, certain analysands are driven masochistically to feel that they are being humiliated, they are likely to feel talked down to no matter how genuinely egalitarian their analyst's manner might be. Either they will not trust that manner or they will take it as conde-scension or weakness. This is not to say that the searching attitude might not receive the same reception; the difference lies in the analyst's inner attitude, which is more stable and ultimately helpful. By virtue of being less presumptuous, the analyst is maintaining a secure emotional base for dealing with whatever ensues. In contrast, the implicitly lofty explanatory posture overexposes the analyst to negative countertransference as the rejected or misused authority who has been acting on fantasies of "benevolent and reassuring" analytic omniscience.

With prepared minds, analysts do, of course, already know in a general way much of what lies ahead before the analysis begins. Nevertheless, when they are analyzing most effectively, they work with no definite expectations as to concrete detail, sequence, fixed context, and the analysand's immediate use and misuse of their interventions. The increased confidence that ordinarily comes with experience helps the analyst maintain conscious alert-ness in a directionless manner. By being ready for nothing in par-ticular, the analyst is ready for anything. In this respect, analysts are in the same position as the Zen pupil who must learn, as part of his training, that the only successful way to ward off the unexpected blows his master inflicts is never to anticipate the direction from which the next blow is coming and when it will come.

## RECALL OF INSIGHT

It is well known that, post-analytically, analysands find it diffi-cult to recall on demand the content of major insightful interpretations or to reproduce precisely clusters of them organized around basic themes; however, they do recall many of these insights when there develop relevant contexts of problematic experience. Consequently, it need not be assumed that, in a deep sense, they have forgotten what they have come to understand. But does our estimate of our work rest on what analysands can later recall spontaneously? I think most analysts agree that that estimate, given reliable information, depends mainly on the transformed way these ex-analysands now construe their lives and, in their new terms, are living their lives less self-injuriously and otherwise more adaptively. Analytically, mere behavioral change "for the better" is not conclusive evidence. It might be a defensive move. What matters is its meaning or its function.

De-emphasizing recall as *the* test of integrated insight rests on the premise that the insight is for us, the analysts. For us, remembered and revisable insight is the constant; for the analysands, it is the variable. Instant recall, as though of a well-learned lesson in school, is not the most convincing sign of retained benefit after an analysis is concluded. However, it is the case that, as the analysis continues, analysands do usually manifest more stable conscious grasp of the insights achieved, they preserve them more accurately than they could earlier, and they do not try to control the analyst's memory (see Chapter 4).

## CORRECTIVE EMOTIONAL EXPERIENCE?
## NEW OBJECT?

In recommending this searching attitude, it is not my aim to provide the analysand with a corrective emotional experience (in my opinion, a concept of doubtful value owing to its discounting the continuing role of unconscious, unrealistic fantasy in the transference). Rather, I am recommending leaving space open for the analysand's active collaboration as a co-creator or co-author of mutual understanding. Of course, the analysand is more likely to develop increased trust in an analyst whose manner is genuinely searching and show this by becoming more open; and so much the better, provided that this development is not then used collusively by both participants to bypass inevitably lingering mistrust, envy, and antagonism. On the other hand, as I mentioned, the analyst's unassuming attitude might be experienced negatively, for example, as a ploy to induce one to let down his or her guard in relation to someone who might well be harboring persecutory intentions.

Nor am I recommending a one-sided stand on the issue of the analyst as a "new object" in the sense often wrongly ascribed to Loewald (1960): not a benign figure taken as such by the analysand whose presence is necessary for the process to move forward, nor a figure whose existence is the result of the analytic process after the analysand has withdrawn many of the previously necessary projective identifications. As an alternative to these two explanations or goals and in the sense I believe intended by Loewald, I propose that it is more useful to envisage a dialectic process whereby the analysand, bit by bit, takes hold of a bit of insight or some other sign of empathic interest and feels readier than before to incorporate more insight or to take a chance on and tolerate more engagement than before, and so on. Increasingly, the analysand is capable of sufficiently improved reality testing within the analytic relationship to recognize the analyst as just that—an analyst. Accordingly, I recommend viewing the "new object" analyst primarily as a figure who both develops during the process *and* progressively enables the process to go forward. That is to say, the analyst as analyst steadily becomes more of an enabler, and so is at one and the same time a condition of analysis and its result.

## CONCLUDING REMARKS

This second chapter on insight has been devoted to showing that reconsidering the question, "Insight for Whom?" raises significant technical and conceptual issues. I believe my discussion of this question can help free us from the lingering effects of what I regard as Freud's somewhat intellectualistic and overeager bent toward explanations that were to his satisfaction at least. Although we are now in a position to regard this tendency as appropriate for a genius engaged in developing the extraordinary clinical and theoretical discipline that psychoanalysis is, we can also see that it was not ideally suited for engaging ambivalent analysands in the difficult work of maintaining a collaborative analytic dialogue and moving through their complex mazes of conflicts and fantasies.

# 3

---

# Insight: Seeing or Telling?

Our everyday language and our psychological and philosophical language are saturated with visual-spatial metaphors for thinking, rethinking, understanding, and sometimes even communicating. For example, we say, "I see what you mean," "In this perspective," "Introspect," "Think deeply about it," "Reflect on it," "Get your point across," and "A colorful account of the incident." These are not dead metaphors. I will try to show that this is so by giving an account of the influential role they continue to play in psychoanalytic theorizing and clinical interpretation. I will lay out some theoretical implications of our using the term *insight* to refer to psychoanalytic understanding of our "inner" and "deeper" selves and those of other human beings. Additionally, I will detail some of the technical consequences, both advantageous and problematic, of our formulating interpretations in ocular terms.

Here, we are concerned particularly with the metaphor insight. It is so deeply embedded in ordinary language that it may be said to have been naturalized, that is, to be no longer regarded as figurative speech but only as a way of talking plain talk. Now, when modes of discourse have received so much critical attention, it no longer seems self-evident that analysts must continue to depend on metaphors of looking and seeing when discussing psychoanalytic understanding. This being so, one must ask, "What accounts for the lasting appeal of these metaphors?"

To deal with this question in relation to insight specifically, let us begin with another question, one that is more consequential than it sounds initially. If we ask, "What do we see into when we develop insight?" we must answer that we see into nothing at all because we are not looking. We are thinking, and we are using a visual-spatial metaphor to tell that mental action. Even if certain aspects of our thinking might be best described as visualizing (for example, dreaming), the visualizing can be regarded as staging an as yet unverbalized, unorganized, perhaps repressed and metaphor-rich narrative of subjective experience.

Although I cannot hope to explain fully the appeal of visual-spatial metaphor, I can offer a few sets of possibly explanatory comments. First, the etymology of many of our words roots them so deeply in the physical world of things, movement in space, and sensory qualities—in general, the concrete mode and matter of existence—that it is reasonable to think that, as we learn language, we become predisposed to adopt a physical slant on our thinking and speech. Even the words for our "rising above" the concretely given, such as *reflection* and *introspection*, do not remove us from the visual-spatial world. Note, by the way, my recourse to "remove" and "slant."

Secondly, Freud seemed to have been inclined to accept this linguistic state of affairs when he proposed that the ego is first of all a bodily ego (1923, p. 26). Many analysts continue to follow Freud's lead even after they take into account the conclusion drawn from recent developmental research on attachment that purports to show the primacy of object relations. It now seems to be required to try to work with both ideas simultaneously.

Thirdly, further weight is added to analysts' preference for sensory figuration by Freud's (1915b) correlated emphasis on the concreteness of unconscious mental processes and its clustering around erogenous zones and modes as well as the senses. Ordinary language, on which Freud drew frequently, supports this turn of thought; for example, we speak of smelling a rat, listening with the third ear, feeling things in our bones, jumping out of our skins with fear, a person's being a pain in the ass, someone else's saying a mouthful, and taking distance from a problem. Each locution implies our relying on physical modes of knowing or telling what is the case. Here, we may be not only following the lead of those from whom we first acquired language but also drawing on the pleasure possibilities of imagery. All told, it seems that the converging influence of models, theory, and ordinary language leads analysts to favor metaphors featuring that which can be located in space by being apprehended through the senses, especially sight.

Finally, a sense of the real and true attaches to that which is seen in space, while, in contrast, the spoken word, being more tied to the speaking subject and thus rooted in subjectivity, seems to offer a less trustworthy account of whatever is the case. We know, too, from self-observation, that we do not always tell others about the people and events in our lives frankly and consistently. Consequently, one would want to know the narrator's aims, values, or point of view.

It can therefore be assumed that we analysts have overlearned the physicalistic, implicitly positivistic conceptualization of insight. Insight has remained our term for "really" getting beneath the "surface" of things that are "out there" in the "external world" and "gaining access" to "entities" that are "in there" in the "internal world."

## NARRATION

Nevertheless, it can be argued that all the while we have been mainly trafficking in words selected and arranged to tell and retell stories of past and present lives. That is why I have been proposing for some years now that it accords better with our clinical practice to say that we have been doing our work in the realm of narration (1983, 1992). That much of that narration deals with events and persons in space does not make it any the less an act of telling. Spence (1982), apparently working within the empiricist-realist tradition and so developing his argument differently from mine, which is in the hermeneutic tradition, has also come to a narrativist conclusion.

I suggested earlier that referring to narration stimulates uneasiness because in large measure it suggests that what follows consists of words, words, words, with "nothing" tangible "right there" or potentially presentable "in front of one's nose." In contrast, ocular metaphors strongly suggest unmediated physical presence. Consequently, the first point that must be made against this narration bias is that narration does not necessarily denote creating fictions, imagining things, disregarding the truth-value of what can be concretely apprehended, and, on this basis, being required to adopt a crudely relativistic "anything goes" attitude. Careless use of the word *narration* causes confusion. Results are different whenever that term is used rigorously, as when I maintain that, whatever might be the case in the world, it cannot enter discourse without being thought and told in words or in conventional gestures that serve as verbal equivalents. When we think, we are telling something silently. We may speak our narrative, as when we offer thought-through interpretations, and in speaking we may revise the way we tell our thoughts to give them more form or impact. In our analytic interventions, we are retelling what our analysands seem to have been telling us explicitly and implicitly, specifically when they are associating, recounting dreams, reacting to details of past and present analytic sessions, squirming, and so on. Sometimes, an interpretation is not so much retelling as it is telling for the first time and in an analytically informed way a hitherto unformulated or unorganized meaning of an event or the personal significance of a subjective experience (see also Stern 1997). In these instances, we and our analysands often refer to "finding the words for it."

Whether telling or retelling, the narratologically oriented analyst is not denying the existence of a real world. That orientation does not manifest philosophical idealism, and it does not entail rampant relativism. What is being claimed is that facts exist only under a description. There is no way to deal with the facts of the case except through versions of them. The world as a subject for reflection must be told. Subjective experience cannot be analyzed without being narrated.

Assessing the truth-value of what is told is another matter. It can always be assessed by using the methods and criteria that are accepted within the realm of knowledge and belief in which one is operating. This is so even if the assessment is approximate and even if the result is considered provisional, that is, acceptable for the time being but subject to modification or rejection as findings accumulate and new approaches are developed and accepted. Whichever versions are in play are contingent. Also, the narrator is fallible and must be understood as acting in accord with specific interests and values. One can always ask why one particular version is being constructed.

Further, more than one version of an event can be judged to be provisionally true or factual because each narrator is situated in only one of a number of possible positions. In our daily existence, we take for granted our encountering differing and revisable versions of the "same" true or real event, person, or subjective experience. We ourselves have narrated more than one version of most things in our personal worlds, and we do not then regard ourselves as making up fictional beings, events, and qualities, our being unreliable informants, or our adopting an "anything goes," totally relativistic position. Adaptive living requires this flexibility, for the contexts in which we function vary, and usually we match our discourse to our circumstances. Among other human achievements, reciprocity in thinking and empathy call for this flexibility.

Not to be forgotten in this connection is our realization that perception is most usefully regarded as a process of construction. What is "right in front of your nose" is not self-evident. It is not the same for all observers. What is perceived is a function of where one is standing, the interests and values being served, the perceiver's preparation to see certain things in particular, and many other factors rooted in culture, personal development, and present needs and circumstances. That is what is meant by saying that what is perceived is always mediated. It is erroneous to think that seeing is believing while telling and reading are to be regarded with skepticism. Perception does not provide unmediated and infallible access to a mind-independent, material world that is knowable in some pure, godlike way. Perception is mediated by beliefs about the world and the expectations they generate and also by the narrative formats that are felt to be suitable for apprehending and communicating the naturalized world or creating new ones.

Psychoanalysts often formulate the way they work and their "findings" on the untenable basis of unqualified positivism—the "seeing is believing" orientation to truth and fact. They do not regard themselves as dealing in contingent beliefs and observations inseparable from narrative commitments. They adopt this positivist stance toward "nature"—itself another construction according to the present argument and not a directly apprehended set of fixed entities. Thereby, these analysts disregard a large and major part of the history of epistemology and science, doing so possibly to feel more confidence while working their way through the myriad ambiguities typically encountered in practice.

In their clinical work, however, analysts typically do not function as philosophical realists, though they may talk as though they do, as by preferring "it is" over "it seems" and "it must" over "I believe." In the fine details of their work, analysts usually function in what I regard as a more epistemologically sophisticated way. They vary their attributions of meaning and significance of what conventionally might be called the same facts, be they actions, personal qualities, or situations. For example, the "same" action might be described as frightened in one context, destructive in another, and self-protective in a third, and each version may have considerable truth-value so far as can be judged at that time by the two participants or by independent judges, such as supervisors or readers of published reports. For them, the reality of each might not be in question; what matters is the most efficacious way in any one context to construct one's interpretive narrative of the analytic issue under consideration.

Thus, the analyst tolerates what might be regarded as contradictory versions of things. Depending on context, the same man can be discussed as a good father, a bad father, an absent father, and so on. In its context, each version can be more or less truth-indicative. In these instances, analysts concerned with being scientific might then resort to using terms like overdetermination, as Freud did regularly, as though referring to simultaneously operating, empirically discovered facts of the case, but in doing so they obscure the hermeneutic process by which they are developing different and believable accounts of whatever is getting to be understood. That is to say, a variety of meanings are accumulating in the analyst's multicontextual thinking. According to this conception, introducing the term *overdetermination* seems to express epistemological misunderstanding based on a sweeping precommitment to deterministic science.

## INTERPRETATION

How do these considerations of insight enter into our interpretations and then affect our analysands? It should be obvious from what has come before that we can expect analysands to have already been thinking about themselves and others in terms that are freighted with visual-spatial metaphors and, further, that when their analysts use these metaphors in the analytic dialogue, they are more likely to connect with unconscious fantasies than when they rely on interventions organized around relatively more abstract, disembodied verbal terms. Consequently, analysts who refer to "the internal world," who say, for example, "the feelings you bury within yourself," "your mother's voice rings in your head," "the two parts of you are at war," and so on are not likely to provoke any confusion or hesitancy other than that connected with defense and negative transference. In one case, using previously disclosed material, I said to one analysand who was telling me that he could not stand to look at himself in the mirror, "You look at yourself through your mother's eyes," and his response made it plain that we were in good communication.

Clinically, the visual-spatial metaphors serve us well, but do they continue to do so if we use them alone up to the end? We need not worry about this eventuality, for ordinarily analysands present and re-present their understanding in terms that have a place in ordinary rational discussion, and on our part we often and appropriately join them in doing so. And it is well that we do so because formulation in verbal, rational form is intrinsically less fluid and so more fit to be a reference point for continuing adaptive efforts (Loewenstein 1956). The issue here is that the concrete metaphors—seeing things, hearing internal voices, feeling sensorimotor changes, and so on—will, as they should, also be strongly represented in the analyst's interventions. That way the analysand is not implicitly encouraged to ignore the interpreting analyst's orientation to the seemingly tangible internal world of unconscious mentation, which is the world of things that we believe plays so large a part in all our lives.

The rational dialogue concerning the concrete, often bodily terms of insight is important in yet another respect. Not only does rational dialogue facilitate remembering, organization, and other benefits of thinking in secondary process terms; it plays a vital part in developing perspective and reciprocity in human relationships. Although *in its concrete aspects*, insight does refer to others insofar as it is considered intrinsically object-related, its major terms are so much in the service of the paranoid-schizoid position that too often they tend toward anxiety, mistrust of others, and alienation from a world experienced, largely through projection, as dangerous; thus, it may be considered insufficiently socialized and sometimes antisocial, and its primitive, part-object, narcissistic qualities limit its potential for contributing to the development and maintenance of mutual, constructive relationships with others.

Therefore, interpretation's effectiveness seems to depend on its dual nature: irrationally concrete and rationally social at the same time. In this respect, we might recall Freud's (1915b) having emphasized the unconscious meanings associated with all conscious thought and also his having attributed special creative achievements to an unusual confluence of contributions from the systems Unconscious and Conscious. There is ample reason to include significant interpretations among these special creative achievements.

## CONCLUDING REMARKS

By continuing to use the word *insight*, I have tried to make it plain that I do not advocate rejecting the term; rather, I have been trying to increase awareness that the communication of insight is grounded in the visual-spatial, concrete metaphors that give narrative form to unconscious fantasies, especially those inferred to be at play in the psychoanalytic dialogue. On this basis, insight may be regarded as a strongly felt and psychoanalytically penetrating narrative of one's own life in the past and present and of the lives of significant others, which is to say that the necessary conditions for emotional insight are being met. In developing my argument, I have tried to show that these further linguistic insights into insight have technically useful applications in the analytic dialogue.

# 4

---

# Remembering in the
# Countertransference

In a letter he wrote in 1938, Walter Benjamin said of Franz
Kafka, "There is nothing more memorable than the fervor with
which Kafka emphasized his failure" (1969, p. 145). I suggest that
in one of its aspects that fervor expressed Kafka's desire to control
his listener's memory of him, specifically to obliterate any record
of Kafka's positive attributes and achievements. Not a victim; a
failure!

Analysts frequently encounter analysands of this sort. After
dwelling on their general unhappiness, these analysands zero in on
their disappointment in themselves, and in the course of belaboring
that feeling, they bring the sense of failure into the transference.
Sooner or later they proclaim themselves failures at analysis and re-
sign themselves to being disappointments to their analysts. In their
role of therapeutic washouts, unconsciously they are trying to make
themselves memorably unapproachable.

This chapter is primarily about these analysands. It conceptu-
alizes them as trying to take possession of their analysts' memories

and erase whatever might have been registered therein as hopeful, encouraging, or promising. To ensure the success of their project, they are intolerant of their analysts' having memories of their own; that is, their being psychically separate and different human beings who are able to remember autonomously. They aim not just at eliminating information they might have given from early on in their analyses about personal resources, achievements, and potentials; also in their sights are experiences they have had in their analyses, some of them recent, some even in the session under way, and anything else that might help their analysts remember them as anything but failures. They require their analysts to be so preoccupied with accounts of failure as to effectively surrender control of this most important ego function: remembering.

## REMEMBERING

Remembering plays an essential role in establishing, developing, and enriching those crucial contexts of meaning that both enable insight and interpretation and are the products of the understanding they develop. These contexts are not merely repositories of information or past dialogue; they are tools of analytic work and, as such, agents of ambivalently regarded change. They are needed to maintain continuity and coherence of thought and emotion. Without them, there can be no sense of the past, the present, or the future. Analysts who suffer this ego impairment in the countertransference cannot effectively analyze *that* and *how* these analysands are structuring their transferences and experiencing their relationships, such as they are under these primitive conditions; nor will these analysts be able to cope with developments in their countertransferences, for they will be dismayed anew at each of their analysands' dismal self-presentations, feel that they are being confronted with irremediably deficient or ruined lives, and suffer impairment of their capacity for reflection.

Some of these assaults on remembering are short-lived, some long. Some countertranferential loss of control over remembering is brief and some is not. I am describing a more or less fluctuating state of affairs. It must be borne in mind that some of the flux in counter-transference need not have been primarily provoked or desired by the analysand; the analyst's self-induced countertransference ten-dencies might be the primary factors in making it hard to remember what is best not forgotten. For example, a male analyst might not remember a major interpretation he made the day before because it touched on guilt feelings he shares with his male analysand, or per-haps he will forget how that interpretation impacted that analysand because he finds it stressful to realize how important he is to him.

When analysts have their own significant insecurities about success and failure, they can all too readily fall into the transfer-ence-set trap of assuming the role of judge—benignly reassuring or demandingly confrontational—and enter into frequent or pro-longed enactments that seriously disrupt the analytic process. When these lapses are detected and controlled early, however, they can be put to good use, the analysts then becoming alert to how their analysands are playing on them, apparently doing so, as analysands will, after having detected countertransference vulner-abilities in the realm of success and failure. So one often observes, when supervising candidates, not to say work of one's own at times.

The analysand's part in these transactions will give evidence of the extent to which he or she is either lodged in the paranoid-schizoid position or has moved significantly toward or into the pre-cincts of the depressive position. Our next step, therefore, should be a short discussion of remembering in relation to these two funda-mental psychical positions.

## THE PARANOID-SCHIZOID AND DEPRESSIVE POSITIONS

In analysis, not taking responsibility for one's life proves to be an especially important component of fervent failure. In dynamic importance it ranks well above using self-abnegation to solicit reas-surance or rejection. Other analysands do take responsibility, and they function differently. They, too, are bound to have "failures" of various sorts on their minds, and ordinarily their analysts are prepared to give them room to remember and reflect on these "failures." However compromised their efforts may be, those who are reflective try to understand, to apportion responsibility, to improve themselves, and to make amends in relation to whatever guilt they are prepared to acknowledge. In these respects, they function more or less within the depressive position. They are ready for the sometimes painful burdens of responsibility.

In contrast to these relatively responsible analysands stand those featured in this chapter: those with the Kafkaesque fervor to be remembered as failures. For the most part, they may be said to be in the relatively immature paranoid-schizoid position as described by Melanie Klein (1946). Either they have never progressed significantly beyond this position to a significant degree or they have reverted to it during times of stress and personal disequilibrium. Although many analysands fluctuate between this unreflective position and the more mature depressive position (Anderson 1996, Britton 1985, Klein 1940, Segal 1957, Steiner 1993), more than a few are likely to lodge themselves between the two, that is, to lock themselves into one of those pathological organizations that John Steiner (1993) has characterized as psychic retreats. In these retreats, which are organizations of defenses, sadomasochistic fantasies, and other simultaneously self-protective and gratifying operations, they do not independently make or sustain definite moves in the direction of either of the two painful positions described.

The designation of a paranoid-schizoid position implies a predominantly narcissistic organization of the personality. That organization is constituted in large part by unconscious fantasies of omnipotent self-sufficiency, unreflective or concrete thinking in emotional matters, and envious and sadomasochistic interaction with others in both the internal world and the surrounding world; it also implies much use of defensive splitting, projective and introjective identification, denial, and idealization. This defensiveness fragments and keeps fluid and concrete the content and boundaries of self and others. These analysands cannot deal directly with their ambivalences consciously. Either subtly or obviously, they try to limit communication with others to self-referential, socially isolated monologues rather than engaged dialogues. Under these conditions, the ego function remembering is seriously impaired, most prominently in the transference as manifest, for example, in vehement usage of the words "always" and "never."

By persisting in remembering autonomously, analysts remain understanding observers of the fervent failure that these analysands parade before them. They do not become over-involved participants in these parades. They avoid countertransference retreats from the relatively mature depressive position—retreats either to an early phase of the depressive position in which there is great susceptibility to guilt and atonement or to the thoroughly immature paranoid-schizoid position.

The analyst who does not retreat in response to her or his analysand's fervent fantasies or demonstrations of failure will be able to go on to remember periods, however brief, of significant joint analytic work that manifested some of the analysand's adaptive resources. Whether the analysand has been in analysis for a while or is new to analysis, that analyst will also remain able to remember affirmative life-historical material gathered during initial interviews. He or she will be able to track the rise and fall of fervent failure and so will not develop a static picture of the analysand as mostly or simply a jumble of ruins. By doing so, the analyst will be in a much better position to develop insight into the unconscious fantasies being lived out in the transference.

## COLONIZING THE MIND OF THE OTHER

The analysand who invades and takes possession of the analyst's remembering, however transiently, may be said to be colonizing the analyst's mind. Colonizing seems to be a particularly suitable metaphor to use for the part-object, narcissistic, paranoid-schizoid relationships these analysands tend to form. Just as many of the victims of historical colonizing have been subjected to treatment that causes them to lose heart and so to surrender much of their minds, wills, and memories to their invaders, these analysands try to subjugate their analysts. Then, the analysts remember largely in accord with the program of their masters. Although manifestly the analysts remember their analysands as leading failed lives, it is the analysands who, upon analysis, emerge as the successful oppressors and exploiters.

So long as the analyst remains relatively autonomous, she or he is able to maintain enough distance and perspective to keep trying to develop through interpretation a collaborative but differentiated dialogue aimed toward insight and change. Once colonized, however, the analyst does not remember to persist in understanding what the analysand is up to, that is, what the analysand is showing or hiding each moment defensively, libidinally, or aggressively, and also what he or she is contriving and enacting through compromise formations. That analyst has been blinded to the analysand's conquering the analytic effort through shows of helplessness, hopelessness, suffering, and, most of all, failure. No longer available to the analyst is any clear and consistent appreciation of just how much of the analysand's strength, even violence, has entered into their relationship. However designated— negative therapeutic reaction, negative transference, psychic impotence, or masochistic defeatism—these destructive strategies have subjugated the now fragmented and powerless analyst. Resentment may follow close on the heels of this disempowerment. Fundamentally, then, it is not so much that the analysand has jockeyed the analyst to do the thinking for her or him, as it is that, implicitly, the analysand is doing the thinking for both of them.

The idea of colonizing implies that projective identification has played a paramount role in the attacks on the analyst's capacity to remember autonomously. The invaded analyst is so filled with the analysand's own fear and despair that her or his enterprising spirit has been stifled. Stifling that spirit is one aspect of what Kafka must have systematically set out to do, not only in his writings but in his personal discourse as well. For example, he is reported to have said the following to his friend, Max Brod, who had asked if there was any hope: there is indeed "plenty of hope, an infinity of hope, but not for us" (1969, p. 116). Later on, Samuel Beckett provided a large number of artful versions of this dismal discourse, among which is one somewhere that goes something like this: "All change is a change of muck; still, some change is better than no change at all."

The colonizing analysands' use of projective identification to control their analysts' remembering include a special tactic, namely, depositing in their analysts' minds their own capacities to think and their own thoughts as well. This tactic is suggested by their frequently asserting, "I know just what you are thinking," or "Only you can make some sense of all this." Their goal is to achieve control through establishing a common identity of context and outlook. Then, they hope, it will be possible to avoid having to cope with the immense emotional complexities of otherness in a continuous two-person situation. These unwelcome complexities include not only the dependency, persecutory anxiety, envy, disappointment, and confusion common to the paranoid-schizoid position, but also the dreaded loss, guilt, and burden of reparation entailed by approaching the depressive position. When there is only one mind in the room, life is simpler even if still consciously painful. I will soon present some clinical examples of these difficulties.

Consequently, the analysand's projective invasion and control of the analyst's remembering can be said to take the heart out of efforts to remember otherwise and to leave in its place a censored text. Among themselves, analysts do speak, on occasion, of losing heart or being disheartened. When they do, it is time to ask whether an analysand with Kafka's fervor has successfully projected temporary amnesia or spotty recall into the countertransference. In contrast, when that analyst is not in the grip of dismal countertransference, he or she is more likely to respond to these invasive, controlling efforts by thinking relatively calmly that perhaps a way has not yet been found to establish an analytically effective dialogue, that one is stymied, that at present the analysand's defenses seem to be too strong to allow the work to move ahead, or that the analysand feels too threatened to say anything.

## CLINICAL EXAMPLES

*First example.* Ellen, a young teacher, had been in analysis for a number of years and had benefited from our joint work to the extent that she had significantly modified her characterologically rooted patterns of demeaning herself and causing herself to suffer and perform poorly through obliviousness, blundering, vagueness, helplessness, and fearfulness. At the time of the event to be reported, Ellen was a more developed person than she had been: interpersonally, professionally, and in her inner life. She was more resourceful, independent, and able to gain recognition for her previously hidden assets.

As expected, she had not utterly renounced her former ways. Both in the transference and in her external affairs, she occasionally plunged herself into painfully humiliating circumstances. At times it was clear that these self-injurious shifts expressed defensive reactions that combined envy, spite, and continuing fears that further gains would inflame her narcissistic parental figures, often represented now by me in her transference; I would be inflamed to the point of punishing her by abandonment. To Ellen, it would be the very abandonment she had experienced as a child.

Having always dreaded being left "all alone," she readily imagined herself to be actually alone in the transference. For example, she experienced my absences over weekends or holidays as painful and hateful withdrawals and abandonment. Absence, she felt, was clearly in the service of my narcissistic social and sexual pleasures. At the time I am about to discuss, these reactions were no longer so regular and so extreme as they had been, but they did recur when she felt under great stress.

The immediate context of the occasion to be considered here was this: Ellen had recently improved a close relationship of long standing, she had changed jobs, and she had bought a needed car that she could afford with the help of scrimping. The analytic context included preliminary discussions of termination; it was beginning to be a thinkable prospect. Each of these changes had been accompanied by brief, repeated defensive reactions directed against her and me. The precipitating issue was a pending national holiday that included a long weekend.

At this time, Ellen became increasingly depressed, tearful, and complaining. She dwelled on how helpless, frightened, and alone she was. She filled her sessions with this defensive material to the point where she began to seem determined to overwhelm me with guilt for abandoning her in so sorry a state. This was a guilt I would feel were I to forget completely how *not alone* she actually was, how resourceful and resilient she had proved herself to be over the past few years, and how spitefully, enviously, and self-destructively she was responding to the "aloneness" she now connected with the idea of termination. She was experiencing the long weekend as the harbinger of that dreaded event. I was able to remember all this well enough to begin to interpret this reaction.

Nevertheless, I began to notice that her distraught yet unconsciously attacking self-presentation was getting to me. I caught myself thinking irritably, "Not again!" In that thought was the implication that I believed that I had good reason to insist that she remain securely beyond all such reactions to separation no matter what the context. I realized that she was controlling me to the point where I was beginning to forget my knowledge of her and my sense of myself as her analyst. Even in the midst of interpreting along this very line, I was losing my grip on my own resources for interpretation. I realized further that my irritability was in the service of staving off some tinge of countertransference guilt. Ellen helped me reflect on my reaction: using her analytically hard-won capacity to form and express convictions of her own, she complained that an irritable tone of voice had crept into some of my preliminary interventions.

Consequently, I was able to put the matter to her in the following way. I told her that I believed she was reverting to her old way of being: emptying out the life she had begun to live so that she could feel depleted and alone, thereby creating a basis to rebuke me and make me feel guilty in reaction to her show of being in a pathetic, abandoned state. She hoped to succeed in getting me to forget all the personal resources and resilience she had been enjoying of late. In response to this much, and in a further enactment of her display of helplessness, she took these remarks, the substance of which was not really new to her, and began to mangle them so badly that she had trouble grasping and retaining what it was that I was pointing out. In this way she showed how much she was once again project-ing into me her own capacity to think and how destructive she felt. In keeping with my estimate of her present resources, however, I decided not to intervene further at this point. Recalling her gains of recent times, I had been letting her be more on her own in the ses-sions, that is, letting her grope her way towards independent under-standing. I was convinced that if I acted otherwise, I would lead her to experience me as worrying about her or trying to control and rep-rimand her, in either case inducing her to revert to infantile pat-terns of behavior as her mother had done.

So, I simply continued to listen, and slowly she began to "get it" so that, by the time the session was ending, she had a pretty good idea of what I had said. The next day she showed that she had re-covered a lot of her lost ground (not so much *lost*, really, as ruined and repressed spitefully). Then, she was able both to remember clearly enough the points I had made and to go on by herself to express directly her spiteful feelings of wanting to make me suffer before I left. I was to suffer because, as she said, I could just go off without her for my own pleasure; in retaliation she was going to "fix me good!" In a shift back to her hard-earned, more adaptive posi-tion, Ellen then began to reflect on the meaning of her outburst: she was experiencing the extended weekend not only in its own right but also as a preliminary termination.

Insightful though it seemed, this much alone could have been submissive compliance designed to cling to me. However, during the next week Ellen was able to analyze our encounter further. She brought out this additional aspect of her rage: she resented my re-cently increased restraint within the sessions because it signified

to her that I was abandoning her in preparation for an abrupt termination. She felt all this even though, consciously, she had been
valuing and enjoying her recently gained sense of competence and
freedom. Also, she knew nothing had yet been decided about termination. Moreover, she could see that her pre-weekend retreat into
resentful defensiveness had shown her to be shifting away from taking responsibility for her own decisions and pleasures and their consequences and that she had been doing so in order not to face being
separate and different from me. Ellen went on to explain that she
was again equating separateness with aloneness and abandonment
and not with entering into that genuine sense of a two-person relationship that the two of us later defined as "being together."

Although this report of a clinical sequence illustrates a number
of important factors involved in transference when termination is
in the air, I have used it mainly to develop one version of the material, namely, Ellen's trying to take possession of my memory of the
analytic process and destroy it, leaving me then preoccupied with
both my resentment and my guilt at having caused her seemingly profound and innocent distress over the coming holiday weekend. My
passing state of irritation showed that I had been colonized briefly,
and my subsequent cooling off had been effected not by me alone but
by the two of us working jointly.

*Second example.* Tom had benefited sufficiently from analysis to
have just changed jobs; from the standpoint of pay and professional
recognition, he had moved up in the world. One day he arrived for
his session agitated and frightened. Slowly he began to acknowledge
anger with me as though his life change had been undertaken in
submission to me. Tom went on to complain bitterly that he didn't
want a man's job; he still felt like a boy, and he wanted to stay that
way. He protested, "This whole thing is your fault!" At this point in
the analysis, this persecuted reaction to any advancement had been
analyzed repeatedly. Accordingly, I decided to wait for the storm to
pass, which it slowly did, whereupon he began to recall the bright
side of the job change. This was the side that he had been able to
keep in focus during the time when, with difficulty, he had been ar-

ranging the change. The session illustrated what, from the stand-point of defense analysis, I call, "first, the bad news" (see Schafer 1992, pp. 195–204).

In one of its aspects, Tom's move towards immaturity was a narcissistic power play to control my remembering. He was trying to get rid of his own ambitions and improved self-esteem by using projective identification in the transference. On that basis he could then think of himself as merely complying with my wishes. He hoped that this would help him avoid experiencing the psychic pain of ambivalence over his responsibility in effecting the change. His ambivalence stemmed from his hoping to avoid experiencing a sense of loss in connection with giving up another piece of his life-long psychic retreat into masochistically colored boyhood. Were he to have succeeded in his colonizing effort, he would have had grounds to expect me to lose perspective and begin to worry that he had moved ahead in his occupational life too fast. Then, I would assume the responsibility for his having done so, and I would realize that he was being dominated by my ambitions for him. Were I to have absorbed the projective identification and reacted this way, I might then have been tempted to act as an advocate of the change in a guilty and defensive manner, for instance, by taking the lead in bringing up the adaptive aspects of his professional move forward; however, in that case I would have been colluding with his defensive strategy and ceding control to him.

In this example, we can also see how taking possession of my remembering could have affected the ego function of anticipation. Specifically, Tom's future would have been crowded out of the picture, for in making the job change, he was taking steps to build a future that, in earlier sessions, he had begun to envisage hopefully and with some confidence, albeit still with some conscious anxiety, resentment, and sadness. Indeed, it had been one of his objectives in coming into analysis to overcome his professional inhibitions. In part, he was aiming to erase a better future from my mind, too, thereby enacting Kafka's "plenty of hope . . . but not for us" (1969, p. 116).

*Third example.* A young woman, Jean, previously depressed, and now in a somewhat more hopeful state, had begun cleaning out her closets, bookshelves, and bureau drawers to make room for the new books and clothes she had been acquiring in connection with her having become sufficiently organized and motivated to begin living a life that was more social and intellectually challenging than had been the case earlier. She had begun to appreciate her attractiveness and her intellectual capabilities. She found the process of divestiture especially painful because it signified to her severing even more of the bonds with her oppressive and infantilizing parents. She anticipated exposing herself to all the burdens of loss, guilt, and aloneness that are stirred up by that transition to adult life. Fearfully, and in disregard of the obviously heartening changes in her recent life, she was dwelling in one session on the aloneness that was in store for her.

Jean went on complaining in such an intense, unremitting way that I found I had to struggle to keep my bearings on what pertained to her tendency to play on my capacity to remember and what to the expectable burdens of change towards maturity in her internal world. The two go together, of course, but differentiating them has its uses. The gains she had made were not merely impressions that I had formed on my own; she had already documented them convincingly and repeatedly. Thus, even at this clinical moment, when, for defensive purposes, Jean was mounting an invasive assault on me, she was still able to say that she knew intellectually that, in fact, she was far from alone in her new life. Nevertheless, she went on arguing her negative case on the model of the virtually lifelong subjugation and appropriation of her self by her parents. She was trying to convince me that her resulting sense of failure was a necessary and not altogether eradicable part of her existence.

In my countertransference, I had to struggle against a temptation to be the one who did the positive remembering for her. For instance, I thought of contrasting her recent gains with the way she had once actually been. Were I to have done so, I would have been both arguing with her and colluding with her defensive splitting and projective identification instead of analyzing her attempted conquest of my remembering. I would have been retreating with Jean to the paranoid-schizoid position, and, by abandoning neutrality through voicing hopefulness, I would have been taking sides in a way that would have put me exactly in her parents' role. Then it would be as though I was the one who was trying to colonize her. Aware of my temptation, I mostly let her thrash it out by herself, which she did at that time, though only to a limited extent.

My *fourth example* is a collective one. It describes a not-rarely-encountered type of problem: either steadily or at times of reversion to past patterns, an analysand floods the sessions with nonstop talking and changes of emotion. This flooding may be carried on to the point where the analyst cannot follow the material. The individual sentences make sense, and the affects seem appropriate to the immediate content, but the sentences do not hang together and the emotions seem to come and go regardless of their intensity.

For example, one such analysand railed bitterly against the analyst's being unsupportive, then gave a circumstantial account of an encounter with a friend that seemed to have nothing to do with the issue of supportiveness, then mentioned enthusiastically a movie recently seen, then wept over a passionate feeling of love for a child of another friend with whose care she was not at all involved, then . . . then . . . and so on through the entire session and through the next and the one after that. Appropriately, the analyst, whom I was supervising, had been listening for signs of continuity and coherence; however, those signs were not to be found, and after a while the analyst had begun to clutch at straws, looking for any opening to develop an interpretation of transference or defense or even of something displaced from the transference—just to feel helpful and avoid feeling defeated, impotent, and discouraged from trying to intervene. In one respect, he had developed the countertransferential sense of aloneness that I have described elsewhere (1995). By doing the integrative thinking for the analysand, he had been trying to remedy his aloneness by engaging in inappropriate activity.

In instances of this sort, analysts are failing to remember that analytic communication takes place in many ways, not every one of them conveyed in the content of specific sentences or single emotions. They are also failing to remember that impairment of the analyst's ego functions can occur which, while not malignant, may signal that their analysands are engaging in a form of an "attack on linking" (Bion 1959). When that is so, the attack may be directed as much at the analyst's ability to establish continuity and coherence as they are at the analysands' own thinking.

Furthermore, these analysts are failing to remember that these spells of apparent uncommunicativeness might be intended as oblique communications or, if not intended as such, available to be used that way in interpretations. The communication could be that the analysand is feeling utterly fragmented or too frightened just then to be willing to understand or be understood (Joseph 1983). This disruptedness would be based on dread of the painful consequences of remaining, as had recently been the case in the one "flighty" example mentioned, organized at a higher level of functioning and experiencing a sense of relationship to the analyst as a distinct person. These painful consequences can be understood to be the analysand's reacting against these feelings of responsibility and guilt that characterize entering the depressive position.

Often there is also a lurking fear of termination should greater continuity and coherence seem to develop spontaneously. In that case, superficial incoherence may be serving as an early sign of reaction against an immediately preceding period of productive work. That period will have been felt to be leading first to a sense of closeness in the transference and then to abandonment.

In these instances of scatteredness, these analysands have gone beyond trying to cause the analyst to lose track of what has been thought and said earlier in the sessions, including even interpretations that have just been made. They have also begun trying to prevent their analysts from remembering important events and prospects that lie in the analysand's immediate future, such as a brief interruption of the analysis, a visit by an extremely disturbing parental figure, or a pending exciting date that is being preceded by much worry. In contexts of this sort, it is the analyst's job to remember to keep track of the pressure on him or her to become disoriented. It is important not to engage in wild goose chases of the sort described in my example. Although the stimulation of some of these chases may be intended to make a fool of the analyst, other provocations do involve oblique efforts to get something important across to her or him, such as recognition of a regression-based low state of integration.

## THEMES OTHER THAN FAILURE

Thus far I have organized my discussion around Kafkaesque dwelling on failure. There are, however, other themes on which the analysand might dwell in a manner that can, over time, begin to take possession of the analyst's remembering. Success is one of these alternatives. For example, in part, an analysand's steady stream of "progress reports" may be designed unconsciously to get the analyst to forget the severe personality problems that, to begin with, have led to the recommendation of psychoanalysis. Because severe problems are always deeply embedded in the personality, the analyst can expect the analysand to try to spoil all possibilities of change no matter how much they also long for them. Encapsulating these problems in success stories is one such means of spoiling.

Another self-presentation that can begin to control remembering is the analysand's maintaining relentlessly a persecuted posture. In that posture one can readily spoil any and all experiences of rapport, gratitude, love, and responsibility. For example, the analysand repeatedly falls back on charges against the analyst, "You never understood," "You haven't appreciated me," "You've been using the wrong approach," "This has never been helpful," and so on. This analysand will have been using the same defensive strategies in relation to other figures in his or her life. In an analysis that has been moving forward, these charges against the analyst, if sustained over a long period of time, can impair his or her ability to remember other, closer times that included mutual recognition of change for the better. Then the bleak revisionist history of the treatment will begin to seem to the analyst closer to the truth.

Yet another alternative is the analysand's redoubling her or his narcissistic, omnipotent emphasis partly in order to force the analyst to share the illusion that, emotionally, the analysand is entirely self-sufficient. In this instance, the analyst must remain able to think back to all the signs of intense neediness that have been noted since the very beginning of the clinical contact, even when those signs have mostly been implied in the fervor with which the analysand has attempted defensively to exclude them, explain them away, or minimize them. Under this unremitting pressure, the analyst must remember that the analysand's neediness is in the room, so to say; more exactly, the hypervigilant analysand is reacting against a heightened anticipation of feeling needy in the transference.

Last to be mentioned among the alternative themes, though not least and not the end of a complete listing of variations, are the erotized transferences. These include all the assertions, demands, seductive efforts, rages, and depressions centered on the analysand's erotic desires for the analyst. As Freud pointed out in 1914, these attempted erotic invasions probably represent an effort to substitute action for the analysand's remembering and reflective analyzing; unconsciously, they may be designed primarily to lead to the analyst's abandoning the analytic position and entering into an erotic relationship. Here, it is necessary to add that these invasions might also be designed to conquer the analyst's remembering who he or she is, that is, an analyst confronted by the transference and not a supremely desirable human being ideally matched for love with the aroused analysand. Once the analyst is successfully colonized, however, he or she fails to remember the seriousness of ethical responsibility and the requirements of human decency. Also forgotten will be all the signs of hostile feelings in the transference that are now being swept away by the advancing erotic forces. These forces do not eliminate the hostile feelings; as Freud pointed out, they are being subtly expressed in the effort to vanquish the analyst and divest him or her of all authority.

## UNCONSCIOUS OEDIPAL THEMES

A set of interpretations proposed by Ron Britton (1985) and Michael Feldman (1994) seems to apply to some of those situations in which the analysand tries to take possession of the analyst's remembering. These contributors have emphasized the importance of signs that, in the analysand's unconscious fantasy, the analyst may be experienced as a couple or as a member of a community rather than as a single parental part-object that is related exclusively to the analysand. They proposed that the analysand has created a split in the internal world between the analyst and the analyst's mind. The split constructs a triangular emotional situation. This oedipally experienced triangle is supposed to replace the manifestly dyadic relationship.

Then, whenever the analyst consults his or her memory or judgment or understanding, the analysand might experience that action as the analyst's being engaged in intercourse with a third party. Erotic meaning will be projected into that intercourse, whereupon the reflective or introspective analyst with good recall will be experienced as staging a primal scene. The analysand then feels both overstimulated and painfully excluded from participating. All the more reason then for him or her to attempt to seize control of the situation, divide the coupling parental figures, and re-create an exclusive twosome. Colonizing the analyst's remembering and inducing forgetful, unreflective servitude may do this. In a greater psychical shift, there will then be only one omnipotent mind or center of motivating will in the room—the analysand's.

## REMEMBERING AFTER TERMINATION

Termination of analysis does not put an end to the work of remembering (see also Chapter 2). Following Freud (1937), we can attribute this lack of closure to the interminability of analysis. Working through continues for both analysand and analyst, for life always brings new conflicts that reactivate old conflicts and gain much of their force from the ineradicable traces of the painful past. And sometimes, new occasions stimulate what might be called deferred insight.

On the analyst's part, his or her later professional experiences often bring to mind some aspect of past work with other analysands that extends or revises the understanding of that work—again, deferred insight. This remembering might also provide an opportunity to gain insight into the current situation that has stimulated it. For to remember in that way is most likely to express something about the countertransferences and transferences of the moment.

## CONCLUDING REMARKS

Certain kinds of transference can have great impact on the analyst's ego functioning. In certain instances, the primary site of countertransference might be most usefully conceptualized not in terms of fantasies and feelings, but in terms of functional impairments or misapplications. One such effect is impairment of the analyst's ready recall of the analytic material, such as life historical data, the analytic process itself, and his or her role as analyst. Optimally, the analyst strives to continue remembering autonomously by analyzing the analysand's use of splitting, projective identification, and other defensive, manipulative strategies. When the analysand uses these strategies successfully, that is, in an undetected and unanalyzed way, they may be said to be colonizing the analyst's mind.

Although other ego functions are often affected by colonization, remembering is of particular interest owing to its importance in building up and keeping ready at hand the contexts within which balanced and timely interpretations can be formulated with some hope that they will be heard and used effectively by the threatened, fantasy-ridden analysand. Therefore, it helps the analytic work if the analyst keeps a steady focus on several questions related to remembering. First, "How and to what extent is the analysand trying to control my remembering: my remembering the different versions of his or her self-presentation, and of the course of the analysis to date as regards content, conduct, duration, change, and mood?" Also, "Is there a primary emotional coloring or dominating attitude that has been imposed on my remembering, such as discouragement, defeat, low expectation, growing optimism, or gratification of therapeutic zeal?" And a third question: "By the attack on my ability and desire to remember otherwise, is the analysand trying to eliminate any trace of triangularity from the analytic relationship or, in the extreme, any experience of my having a separate identity or being in any way different from the analysand; that is, is an effort being made to eliminate from my memory all traces of a divide between the complex analysand and my own many-sided complexity?"

This mode of listening in terms of assaults on the analyst's autonomous remembrance of things past, present, and future can help avoid analytic impasse. It can be particularly helpful in working through disruptive reactions to therapeutic gains, not only those that occur when apprehensive fantasies of termination begin troubling the improving analysand but also those that threaten to obstruct termination that has already been agreed on. Additionally, it can help sustain the analyst's neutrality in the face of the intense conflicts being interpreted.

# 5

# Intimate Neutrality

Neutrality is no longer a neutral topic. Particularly in recent years, the presumption of the analyst's neutrality has been boldly challenged. The most consequential challenges have been mounted by members of the relational school of psychoanalysis, some of whom now discredit the idea of neutrality totally. Their conception of psychoanalytic theory and technique, which deviates in many important ways from contemporary versions of the tradition established by Freud, leads them to claim that it is dead wrong to hold neutrality up as an ideal, a principle, or even a human possibility. They regard expression of the analyst's personality as being inevitable, which no one would deny, but also inevitably highly consequential in the clinical interaction, and some go on to conclude from this that countertransference is built so deeply into the analytic process and that it would be correct to regard any analytic activity as an enactment (for example, Friedman and Natterson 1999, Renik 1998).

Analysts of other persuasions have had their own problems with this concept, having so often found that they differ among themselves when hearing clinical presentations as to whether the analyst is indeed working in a neutral manner. These differences may be attributed to differences of definition, variations in grasp of theory, specialized clinical experience, and purely personal factors that show up in differing countertransference proclivities.

Whatever the case, the fact of these differences, both large and small, indicates that the idea of neutrality in the analytic situation is ambiguous and unstable. So much is this so that it requires constant rethinking and updating if one is to keep pace with current developments and controversies. Here, in the interest of promoting clarity but with no illusions as to the possibility of achieving a conclusive and comprehensive formulation, much less general agreement, I will take up in sequence what I regard as three of the many major sets of issues to confront when standing up, as I do, for the idea of neutrality as both an ideal and a credible clinical claim:

(1) definitional issues that arise from philosophical commitments, some of them acknowledged and some only implied;

(2) issues of complexity that indicate our need for a multidimensional conception of neutrality in place of the simplified conceptions that are frequently but fruitlessly debated; and

(3) the confusion that results when, as is so commonly stated or implied, neutrality is regarded as antithetical to emotional relatedness.

## PROBLEMS IN DEFINING NEUTRALITY

The traditional psychoanalytic usage of neutrality implies an unacknowledged commitment to philosophical realism. Simply put, that realism affirms the possibility of arriving at a correct, final, and exclusive truth about aspects of a real world; it does not rest on perspectivist, pluralistic, hermeneutic approaches and conclusions about that world. In psychoanalysis, realism stands for establishing *the correct interpretation of the analytic material being considered.* I have already indicated that I consider that realism not appropriate to clinical analytic work in that it presupposes that judgments made about the analyst's attitudinal position in the clinical relationship, together with its antecedents and consequences, can be verified conclusively and exclusively. But, as I shall be arguing, these judgments, being concerned with data that are extremely impressionistic, much of it nonverbal or unverbalized, and therefore subject to widely varied interpretation based on varied assumptions that imply different points of view, cannot treated as factual claims to be subjected to traditional empirical tests and decisively proved or disproved. Being limited to judgments of right and wrong and unable to deal with complex variations, the realist presuppositions cannot yield technically useful applications.

Against the realist conception stands what I regard as the strong argument that clinical judgments of neutrality can be arrived at only hermeneutically. For neutrality is not an essence, such that one might ask what it *is*; the word designates a context-dependent judgment and so can be no one thing. That is to say, far from being a fact about unmediated observations of exactly what is the case, these judgments are interpretations constructed in fluid contexts, so that, in principle and practice, they are never final, total, and exclusive of other interpretations. In part, this inconclusiveness is due to the fact that these interpretations are constructed in specific contexts of theoretical presuppositions, technical aims and methods, and values, both personal and inherent in the analyst's system of thought. As such, they always remain open to challenge from other points of view based on other assumptions and goals. For example, when judgments of neutrality are at issue, colleagues are always entitled to ask, "Neutral within which framework?" "Equidistance (a frequent synonym) by which measurements and for which purpose?" "Neutral in which respects and to what extent?" "Neutral as compared to what?" "Neutral according to whom?"

On this understanding, there is no unambiguous, directly accessible set of attitudes to test, no simply real phenomenon unmediated by these contextual considerations. Each set of claims requires assessment in its own terms. Traditional tests of competing claims cannot do the job, for when differing claims emanate from differently constructed worlds of clinical concepts, practices, and phenomena, they establish conflicting ideas of evidence. No single conclusion can be said to be, as Freud would sometimes say, "compelled."

Considered hermeneutically, each interpretation is an optional, though not entirely free, construction that takes into account a particular version of the total clinical situation and its history. (It is not entirely free owing to its embeddedness in a systematic point of view and the constraints imposed by the need to avoid strange, apparently useless formulations that do not rest on an adequate account of why this departure is called for; for example, calling a smile a sneer without explaining that there is a class of smiles that conveys contempt and condescension.) Constructed interpretations are made in the context of the total clinical situation and its history *as presently understood by the individual analyst*. In contrast, every attempt at measurement by traditional, allegedly disinterested scientific investigators must rest on a necessarily highly reductive procedural manual that prescribes so narrow a point of view on constructing contexts and assessing importance that its relevance to clinical work is, at best, severely limited. Contextless induction is a myth.

Analysts position themselves within various, more or less integrated systems of thought and then attempt to define neutrality in its terms. These definitions are mediated by aims, methods, criteria, values, beliefs, competence as assessed by qualified peers working within the same system of thought, and substantial agreement among peers as to how to construe the material being worked with. In psychoanalysis, this material consists of the analysand's more or less tendentious and often inconsistent and changing narratives of past and present experience, stated explicitly or implied in the flow of associations and enactments, and the analyst's more or less systematic, though perhaps also somewhat personally (countertransferentially) tendentious and changing narrative responses to them. To conclude from this that every intervention by an analyst is an expression of *countertransference* and an *enactment* is to empty two valuable clinical concepts of their usefulness in developing particularized insights and interpretations. So used, these two key words signify not much more than that two living human beings are present in the analytic situation.

Returning now to the argument for a hermeneutic conception of insight and interpretation in general and neutrality in particular, we may consider next the question how best to approach critically one often-repeated idea of neutrality: *neutrality means that the analyst does not take sides in dealing with any of the constituents of the analysand's conflicts.* Obviously, this idea requires us to ask the analyst how she or he conceives each side or component of the conflict. Even within the same school of thought, there are numerous ways to define these constituents. For instance, the account given by any one analyst will depend on whether she or he is describing each component from close up, say, as loathing a specific trait of a specific person, X, or from a distance, say, as "an aversive reaction to X," both cases qualifying as accurate or true statements. The point is that components of conflict do not define themselves. It is always an analyst who defines them and comes to conclusions within a complex context that he or she has constructed by applying an individualized version of some more or less standardized professional orientation that is recognizably psychoanalytic. Among other things, each analyst will have relatively specific criteria of what qualifies as "information" to be used in constructing contexts and the descriptions of the conflicting elements. Here, values may enter the scene unobtrusively. As for the information used, typically it is incomplete, inexact, unstable, not totally transparent or assured of consensual validation, and amenable to different narrative treatments. For these reasons, one analyst's "loathing" might be another's "contempt," and a third's "perfectionism," with the result that their ensuing constructions of interpretive contexts, however similar they may seem, will not be identical. That being so, these constructions will lead to more or less different accounts of the con-flict in question, each certifiably true in its context. Then, like-minded analysts disagree.

To take another example: many psychoanalysts use Freud's structural propositions—id, ego, and superego—as organizing con-cepts. However, a gray area surrounds each of these concepts. The boundaries of each of them cannot be sharply defined in a way that is universally accepted. Additionally, the structural approach recog-nizes the importance of accounting for the mutual relations of these hypothetical substructures of the human mind, and similarly ori-ented analysts do not always see these relations in the same way. Due to these conceptual and interpretive variations, most clinically significant phenomena are not amenable to single, precise, widely accepted structural placement. Structural conflict there may be, but how it is to be defined or narrated remains an open question.

Hartmann's (1960) conceptualization of moral values is an in-stance of this problem. He envisioned these values as falling be-tween ego and superego and sharing properties of both. In so doing, he left room for some analysts to approach an instance of valoriza-tion as pretty much a superego affair and the next analyst to judge it an adaptive, reality oriented conclusion that still bears traces of a moralistic stance and unconscious moral conflict. Consequently, the analyst who, simply on his or her say-so, claims to be making definitive and impartial structural designations of conflict will be neglecting, and might well be avoiding, the questions of how and why the structural issues under analysis at that moment have been worked out and which alternatives have been rejected, why so, and with which consequences. Similarly, some analysts, Freud among them, have placed the ego ideal within the superego while others have regarded it as a separate structure and perhaps one that devel-ops earlier (compare Freud 1923, Hartmann and Loewenstein 1962, Jacobson 1964, and A. Reich 1954); in this instance, too, specifications of conflict will vary and, with it, its interpretive con-sequences. It is not being argued here that systematizing efforts are intrinsically chaotic, but rather that there is room for heterogeneity within systemic constraints. It is a case of freedom within organization or a case of an allowable range of perspectives within the same system.

I indicated earlier that equidistance from the constituents of conflict has been a widely used version of neutrality (A. Freud 1936). This geometric metaphor and its narrative elaborations have been taken to imply impartiality. However, the same challenges as those mounted above must be directed at *equidistance*. For, within the hermeneutic approach that is intrinsic to clinical work, it is inconceivable that there can exist purely objective *psychical* geometry or precise *psychical* scales on which to determine the weight of attitudes. One must raise such questions as "Which criteria of distance are being used and why?" "What constitutes impartiality in each instance?" and "Impartial according to whom?" And so on. And then, to be credible, one must answer only from within a specific systematic position.

Analysts must also ask, "Distance from what?" That "what" might refer to an event, action, or fantasy that, upon examination, will be found to be complex and unintegrated and therefore require further analysis before the idea of neutrality can be brought to bear. For example, that "what" might refer to only one element in an aggregate of split-off part objects or one member of such heterogeneous groups as "parents" or unspecified "others"—those vague designations that hinder the analyst's construction of focused analytic interventions. Similarly, *status* is often envied, but, to be obvious about it, status in the drug community would not be expected to stimulate the same response as status in a psychoanalytic society. And status in either one might signify primarily masculinity in one case and security in a family setting in the next.

It should be quite plain by now why my rethinking of uses of the word *neutrality* without further qualification has led me to the conclusion that they should be considered ambiguous or semantically unstable. Its conceptual analysis is best approached with a readiness to defer clinical judgment and ask a series of system-oriented as perhaps value-oriented questions. To be at all amenable to comparative discussion and assessment, answers to these questions must be framed in system-specific and context-specific terms. But beyond individualized variations in systematically contextualized approaches, there lie other factors to be dealt with when rethinking neutrality. A second factor, and the next to be taken up, I designate *multidimensionality*.

## MULTIDIMENSIONAL LISTENING

Analysts usually listen in more than one way and on different levels. They listen to the multiple ramifications of manifest content, and they also hear these ramifications in terms of the four primary analytic modes: transference, countertransference, defense, and adaptation. Countertransferences might center on manifest content that includes: blatant expressions of love, desire, defiance, contempt, anxiety, depression, grief, or transgression; however, it is more often the latent fantasy content that plays on the analyst's countertransference tendencies. Whatever the focus, the analyst prone to disruptive countertransferences will be introducing additional complexity into her or his listening.

At the same time, analysts may be said to be using relatively standardized modes of listening for latent content. That listening will facilitate one or another kind of empathic understanding of their analysands' unconscious struggles, including their need to influence their analysts by projective identification of unwanted parts of their selves. To this end, analysts must also pay close analytic attention to their own reactions. Careful listening to oneself can significantly reduce the intensity of countertransferential emotionality. One wants to respond sensitively but not excessively (by one or another standard) to richly emotional material.

For example, I listen to an analysand, Sid, rant and rave against liberals for their "politically correct" evasions, euphemisms, and knee-jerk expressions of tolerance. This vehemence is Sid's own knee-jerk response to the political science graduate courses he is taking at a local university. Considering myself politically liberal, I dislike hearing my values attacked so passionately, repetitively, and with what I regard as thinly veiled bigotry; however, being aware of my oppositional reaction does not prevent me from analyzing the transferential significance of these outbursts. As I understand them more fully, I begin to sort out that aspect of them that amounts to an attack on me. Supposing me to be a liberal, Sid is using me to displace feelings about his father, a man of the "too understanding" type, one who, it seems, is neurotically eager to be self-critical, reasonable, understanding, and peacemaking in the family quarrels—according to the stereotype, a "liberal" father. Experienced as such, he is a frustrating figure. By providing no paternal authority to fight against, he steadily reinforces his normally volatile, sporadically unreasonable son's feelings of shame and guilt. I defer taking up the link to Sid's father so that further exploration of Sid's position in the transference and in my countertransference will remain as open as possible.

My analytic aim is to understand Sid and help him understand his conflicts and their origins; however, for a long time my efforts only add fuel to the transference fire, for my impartial listening, my trying to understand him and interpret his emotionality in a balanced and differentiated way, only serves to confirm Sid's fantasy about my "liberal" sympathies. As an interpreter, I am "too damned tolerant and understanding," and, as such, I am part of the problem, not part of the solution.

Among other influential factors in this analysis are prominent anal features. Sid's anality renders him intolerant of ambiguity, disorder, inconclusiveness, and, in the analysis, free association—all easily associated with, on the one hand, "too open-minded liberalism" and, on the other, "shit." I expect, and with the help of interpretation I find, noteworthy background disturbance in his relationship with his mother, much of it organized around anal themes. By lending support to reaction formations against both his generous and hostile feelings, the anal conflicts seem to be not only adding force to his basically conflicted attitude toward "liberalism," but also frustrating him in his studies and social relationships and lowering his mood further.

As a reasonably neutral analyst, I felt no noteworthy inclination during this analysis to try to change Sid's political values. It was not my business to try to use analysis to alter his political orientation by interpreting it as an enclave of negative transference or a manifestation of infantile anality and the other factors mentioned above. Although his retained conservatism seemed to serve those expressive functions, there are also many analytic (as well as liberal) reasons to respect his right to his political opinions, their adaptive potential *for him* being one of them.

Sid had entered analysis to overcome work inhibitions and chronic low mood. I took it as my job to analyze those problems and facilitate Sid's changing in those respects and in whichever other ways his symptoms could be traced to other origins. In response to analytic understanding, his politics might have shifted toward the center; however, considering all the predisposing factors, I never did anticipate that change. In the end, though much else changed for the better—*in his terms, not mine*—he did not change his political orientation. He remained a conservative, although a much less volatile and voluble one. I would say that, to the extent that finally he was helped by my neutral interpretations, he had become a potentially more effective political conservative.

Nothing that has been said so far rules out the possibility that, preconsciously or unconsciously, Sid had detected in my general responsiveness my politically liberal sympathies. For his analysis, however, the important thing seemed to be the way he regularly used these fantasies or plausible "perceptions" for attack as well as for defense and in other ways as well that fit into his transference fantasies. Construing the situation in this way and attending to my own feelings as well as I could, I do not believe that I seriously compromised my neutrality in this analysis—nor did I in the following case, in which politics of quite another sort played a prominent part.

In the analysis of a left-wing activist, Burt, whose values were much in line with mine, I developed the interpretation that, for defensive reasons, he was regularly elaborating suspicions that, being an analyst who was costing him money and analyzing his problems with paying me, I was a bourgeois conservative and so could be expected to undermine his values. I also came to interpret his sociopolitical egalitarian activism as, among other things, a defense against unconscious feelings of deprivation, dependence, greed, and cravings for power. Both the defenses and the warded-off cravings seemed to be strongly reinforced by Burt's having experienced a history of maternal deprivation and weakness of paternal authority. These experienced failures of parenting seemed to have severely limited his confidence in his masculinity and left him fearful of "feminine" tendencies.

Burt's analysis did not seem to have been hindered or facilitated in any obvious way by our common sociopolitical values, none of which I acknowledged openly. As time went on, Burt showed fewer of the initially masochistic and unreliable features with which he had been saddled. Also, his capacity to tolerate mutual dependency and to form and maintain loving relationships improved to a noteworthy extent, just as he wished, though they retained noteworthy lability. He remained an activist throughout the analysis. If anything, he worked more effectively.

I do not present these two analytic summaries as unusual clinical accomplishments. Nor do I imply that threats to neutrality are fully understandable on the level of political values. Well-trained and experienced analysts often, if not regularly, go on doing effective clinical work while hearing much manifest content that either clashes with, or endorses, their social, sexual, political, and family values. They continue looking into this content, when it is appropriate to do so, for the light it can shed on the analysand's structural and dynamic development and the part it plays in the difficulties being presented for analysis, especially in the transference. They maintain this degree of neutrality because it matters very much to them to be effective analysts. Each of them has not only a "work ego" (Fliess 1942) but *work ideals* and an *ideal analytic self* on the basis of which she or he rank-orders functional capacities and puts them to use in ways that enable competent and responsible analysis to continue in the face of values and conduct that, were they to be taken at face value, would be either so personally disagreeable or so pleasing as to preclude insightful interest. The functional capacity to remain neutral in the face of disturbing differences or other trying circumstances should be considered vital to effective analytic work.

In these enabling respects, analysts are not unusual. Other professionals—physicians, lawyers, teachers, nurses, dentists, accountants, and so forth—usually perform their tasks in the same way, although they usually do so in settings that do not promote the intense feelings of the sort generated by psychoanalytic intimacy. Certainly, one encounters interindividual and intraindividual variation in analysts' capacities, like those of other practitioners, to maintain standards and live up to ideals, but that that is so does not lead to the conclusion that relatively neutral analysis cannot be carried out.

Furthermore, it is unwarranted, when discussing countertransference and intersubjectivity, to implicitly portray analysts who claim to maintain a fairly steady neutrality as "really" and inevitably victims of self-misunderstanding or pretenders. That portrayal is based on a formulaic application of the idea that, because personal factors cannot be eliminated, personal factors dominate the analytic process. The burden of proof in each instance is on these critics of neutrality; they must show that the analyst is never working in a sufficiently dispassionate way to arrive at interpretations that are in accord with general principles and are more or less convincing to many like-minded colleagues. To think otherwise amounts to dispensing with ego psychology and its basis in abundant analytic observations of how so many people, analysts included, are able to function effectively and with wide consensual support in life's problematic situations. Certainly, it does not follow logically from one's taking a work problem both personally *and* as a technical challenge that she or he is bound to be so overwhelmed by the personal component that one's performance can rightly be described in its terms alone. Nobody knows better than analysts that mixed feelings can be analytically discerned in all reliably adaptive, ongoing, major areas of life.

## REACTIONS TO THE ANALYST'S NEUTRALITY

It comes as a great surprise to analysands as they begin to move toward the depressive position with some sense of security that they are working with someone who steadily maintains an attentive attitude and is listening closely and mulling over whatever he or she says or does, even says or does without having noticed it or without conscious intention, such as using a certain word or metaphor, shifting position, or changing tone of voice. These analysands are likely to have felt for a long time that no one ever really listened to them or responded from a position that was not primarily and dishearteningly narcissistic. This belief, most likely based on experience that can be authenticated but nevertheless is likely to have been exaggerated by projective identifications and envy, and in any case is powerful and of long life, has usually been put to defensive use. If nothing else, it protects against acutely painful repetitions of disappointment or humiliation. Or if not used defensively, then this outlook has been put to masochistic use, as when it has become a way of rubbing salt in one's wounds by repeatedly confirming that there is no reason to hope that anyone could be interested or that, like Kafka, one cannot possibly deserve the other's attention or respect (see Chapter 4, opening). Or all of the above.

Consequently, the analysand denies the analyst's relatively neutral listening, demonstrated by concerned but impartial responsiveness, or else projectively transforms it into feigned or token interest or believes it is only a mask covering disgust or derogatory attitudes. It takes a long time, much interpretation of transference and defense, much working through, and much attention to countertransference tendencies before these mistrustful and despondent analysands begin to genuinely consider that they are being heard and, what's more, heard in a relatively unbiased, other-directed way, which is to say that they are being listened to, as promised, by a respectful, considerate analyst. In effect, the analyst begins to be recognized as such through the haze of transference.

Further, if we take into account the basic psychoanalytic assumption that repression, old and new, is an ongoing fact of everyone's life, it follows that not only are there aspects of the self that remain or become too difficult to acknowledge, but also that projective identification will be steadily in use to ensure relief from painful self-awareness. Consequently, the analyst cannot expect ever to be completely trusted as a neutral figure, nor can the analyst ever take it for granted that he or she is not stimulating mistrust by projecting to some extent, owing to narcissistic concerns. With this brief summary of one of the most arduous and important aspects of doing analysis, we have returned by another route to the topic of Chapter 1, "Insight into Insight."

It might be argued against this understanding of the analysand's growing recognition of the analyst's relative neutrality that the analysand could just as well be understood to be compliantly suppressing or repressing recognition of the analyst's personal biases and of the analyst's blindness to these biases. Or it might be thought that the analysand, for reasons of his or her own, is idealizing the relationship. Situations of this sort do develop often enough in clinical practice. However, it is unsatisfactory to rest one's case against the analysand's ultimate recognition and belief in neutrality on these observations; doing so fails to give due weight to other observations which warrant the assertion that progress toward the depressive position is a complex matter with many identifying and mutually confirming signs, the mass of which make neutrality a credible claim.

## NEUTRALITY AS A FORM OF INTIMATE RELATEDNESS

Far from being played out in silent remoteness—a view of neutrality sometimes taken by some present-day relational analysts in their criticisms of the Freudian tradition—neutrality may be rightly regarded as a form of intimate relatedness. Typically, however, this relatedness does not in any gross manner take one of the many common social forms of involvement with others. It is not the same sort of intimacy as that found in romantic love or enduring enmity, and it resembles familial love and close social friendship only in certain respects.

In its beginnings, neutral relatedness to the analysand can be no more than a possibility. The analysand is a total stranger. Under favorable circumstances, that possibility grows, though it does not do so rapidly or continuously. The work of interpretation facilitates the development of an analytic sort of mutual relatedness. Developing and maintaining that relatedness imposes great demands on the analyst's capacity to be respectful, curious, patient, and ready to be helpfully empathic in response to a fellow human being in distress, even while being confronted by, and interpreting, her or his hostility, aversion, poisonous envy, mistrust, and other negative attitudes and actions. In this way, the analyst's interpretive work promotes the development of an intensely intimate, though specialized form of neutrality.

The analyst's neutral relatedness neither requires nor even favors direct, yielding responsiveness to the analysand's conscious and unconscious wishes. These wishes are often expressed in demands for sympathy, information, guidance, extra time, reassurance, and other forms of social responsiveness. The analyst assumes that these demands are freighted with potentially disruptive unconscious meanings that are not yet recognized or fully understood and are not balanced and regulated by adaptive aims. It is the business of analysis to define these meanings, bring them into consciousness, and, if possible, facilitate the analysand's capacity to integrate or, if need be, marginalize them. Whatever seems that it might impede this work should be restrained. There are times, however, when the analyst must adapt to such special life circumstances as serious illnesses and accidents and respond flexibly. And there are times so ambiguous that one cannot avoid gambling.

Neutral analysts consistently try to remain analysts, that is, more or less skilled, well-intentioned, self-correcting enablers searching for understanding and striving for constructive mastery of analytic situations (see Chapter 2). So far as possible, they must act on the assumption that, at least unconsciously, their analysands, however mistrustful, also depend on their remaining analytic in the face of every temptation or provocation to act otherwise. Although support for this assumption is not always immediately available, it is not rare to discover that, soon after the analyst breaks the neutral analytic frame, the analysand is feeling anxious, guilty, abandoned, defensively omnipotent, or in some other way showing disrupted analytic rapport (see, in this regard, Feldman 1994, on the effects of reassurance in analytic situations). These observations suggest that analysands desperately count on their analysts' individualized forms of professional consistency. Their capacity to tolerate the analytic method seems to rest on the confidence inspired by that consistency.

Responsiveness to the analysand's demands is not rigorously excluded from the dialogue. The analysand's wishes are not ignored. Rather, the responsive analyst is best characterized as being *prepared to not respond in kind*. Effective responsiveness is made plain by steadfastly attempting to maintain the analytic attitude, to gain understanding, and develop useful interpretations. The analyst is not in an either/or situation of compliance, challenge, or reassurance on the one hand and, on the other, silent and remote refusal. Silent listening is often a great help in getting to understand, for it, too, is a way of intervening, and it can be an essential form of activity. Daily life teems with instances of friendly silence that signify active and close presence. It is the same with interventions limited to a show of sustained interest or curiosity.

As mentioned earlier, there is no guarantee that the analysand will totally believe in the neutrality of an appropriate intervention; nor does the analyst count on that much trust. A commonplace example was provided by a guilty analysand who responded negatively to a neutral interpretation of explicit and obvious signs that she was in conflict about going on with her analysis. She then felt accused of cowardice. Only after her guilt feelings were interpreted and explored was she able to acknowledge her ambivalence about continuing the work. Perhaps she had experienced the initial intervention as impatient because it was ill timed or poorly phrased. Perhaps her ambivalence about continuing should have been taken up as a reaction to some real or imagined provocation by the analyst. Perhaps it was something else. Having at that moment no subjective experience to support these conjectures, the analyst did the best he could, and as far as he could make out, the result seemed helpful to the analysis.

In itself, the analyst's sense of neutrality is, of course, insufficient evidence of impartial intervention and helpfulness. For example, in one instance, it finally became clear that, earlier in the analysis, I had been defending successfully against consciously recognizing irritable and disdainful thoughts and feelings. In another instance, I realized only after considerable new material had emerged that a young woman's rejection of an interpretation was not based on defensiveness, as I had been assuming and actively interpreting; rather, it was analytically useful to regard it as primarily an expression of her newly established sense of freedom. That primacy I had failed to recognize owing to my focusing on some secondary issues still in evidence. Similarly, it often happens that an analysand is first thought to be defensively changing the subject after listening to an interpretation, and only later is it understood that she or he has been using displacement to develop the analyst's point in the terms of other, safer, less intimate manifest content. Response by displacement is a common form of compromise that allows the interpretation to sink in and be further developed at a safe distance from the transference. System-based reconsideration often supports this revised view of the clinical interaction. It helps a lot to regard everything in the session as free association, however else one takes it (for example, scheduling, appearance, gait, and so on).

It does complicate matters further that qualified peers working within the same system might, as mentioned earlier, disagree among themselves as to whether an intervention should be considered neutral. The analyst's testimony on this point will count for something but not everything. Once challenged, a number of alternatives might have to be considered, and in the end it may be impossible to arrive confidently at a single conclusion. A series of interventions over several or more sessions might have to be scrutinized before reaching a provisional decision. Analysts engaged in writing up cases carefully for certification or publication and analysts engaged in research often notice their own previously unrecognized lapses from neutrality. What the analysand has noticed and construed in his or her terms is another matter.

It is in the nature of psychoanalytic clinical work to encounter, tolerate, and do one's best to identify and reduce these ambiguities and belated or disputed recognitions, and always to do so only for the time being, that is, to make do with provisional results. Working provisionally helps greatly in maintaining neutrality, developing interpretations to the extent possible, and, *through interpretation* facilitating beneficial change.

## CONCLUDING REMARKS

Analysts' claims of developing and maintaining intimate neutrality have been subjected to much criticism in recent years. It is possible to take account of these critiques without going to the extreme of submitting to demands that one should dismiss the idea of neutrality as merely a self-deceiving, ultimately disruptive ideal. Ego psychological contributions have provided a rationale for analytic functioning that is relatively neutral or dispassionate and yet intimate in its own way. Everyday life and work in other occupations provide abundant evidence that debunking neutrality requires blinding oneself to the capacity shown by relatively mature, unconflicted persons to do their work competently at times of complex and perhaps intense and intimate emotionality.

That the analysand will discern and react to some of the analyst's personality features and emotional responsiveness is a fact not to be denied, and the analyst must feel free to take into account its realistic aspects and their consequences, but neither should it be forgotten that the analysand's unconscious conflicts and fantasies will elaborate even the keenest perceptions of the analyst in ways that express significant unconscious problems and will do so in a way that a poised analyst can interpret to good effect. To think otherwise is to get so enthralled with the analyst's reactivity and the analysand's perceptiveness as to minimize or implicitly discard the idea that analysts are usually capable of relatively integrated ego functioning. Analysts are not expected or entitled to get so lost in their analysands' unconscious mental processes as to be rightly considered possessed by them. Critics who go that far in arguing against the possibility of relative neutrality are minimizing or discarding the idea that unconscious fantasy plays a major part in the uses to which analysands put the fruits of their perceptiveness in the analytic situation. Thereby, they deny the crucial role of unconscious mental functioning and, with that, the foundations of psychoanalysis.

# PART II

---

# Applications

# Introduction to Part II

The three chapters of Part II take up different aspects of Freud's basic contributions to the place of sexuality in understanding the lives of human beings. Freud's interests extended in many directions, among them the clinical, of course, but also the linguistic and the social, among which telling jokes plays a prominent part. Each of my three chapters takes up one of these interests. The clinical requires no further comment here. The linguistic I take up in two areas that have already received their share of critical examination: male homosexuality and perversion. In these areas I believe I have some useful points to add to what has already been taken up. These are points developed in the context of contemporary critical thought—approaches not available in Freud's time. In the third realm—jokes—I bring together the ego psychological updating of Freud's theory of the comic developed by Ernst Kris and contemporary concerns with the sexual politics implicit in many of our seemingly innocuous and even playful social practices, such as telling jokes.

# 6

## Interpreting Sex

In the early days of psychoanalysis, it was comparatively easy to discuss the interpretation of sex. At that time, so different from our own, the meanings of both sex and interpretation were pretty much taken for granted. Sex, to take that first, was understood to begin with the first three relatively distinct and successive pregenital phases of libidinal organization: the oral, the anal, and the phallic. In the phallic phase, there developed the Oedipus complex and correlative castration anxiety and fantasies, on the resolution of which, under favorable circumstances that promote the formation of superego and the renunciation of oedipal objects, depended the attainment of the fourth phase: the genital phase and normality.

Genitality was considered a relatively conflict-free post-oedipal organization of desire and capacity for heterosexual gratification. The pregenital was believed to survive in sexual foreplay and, through transformation, in sublimation. Genitality was the desirable developmental outcome of the sexual instinctual drive in that, in keeping with Freud's Darwinian ground plan, it guaranteed the survival of the species. From the beginning, Freud (1905b) had committed himself to a sexual psychology that would guarantee that survival. Consequently, reproductive sexuality became the developmental ideal. Homoerotic and other forms of so-called perverse and arrested sexuality were deviations from this ideal, caused by disruptive constitutional and early developmental factors that promote pregenital fixations. Relative to the implied idealization of heterosexual genitality—the "oughtness of it"—and in keeping with conventional sexual morality, unmodified expression of these alternatives could not escape being regarded as disturbed outcomes.

Interpretation, our other key word, was understood at that early time to mean discovering, uncovering, or recovering the defensively hidden, repressed, or disguised sexual motives and meanings that underlie the functioning of otherwise reasonably integrated neurotics and contribute to their symptoms and related disturbances of adaptation. Accordingly, the analytic process was thought to be a matter of disclosing these findings to the analysand, thereby lifting the infantile amnesia, making the unconscious conscious, and explaining the pathological influences in the present of infantile fantasy, experience, and conflict. Enlightening the analysand brings relief from neurotic problems. There is self-censorship or resistance to overcome, this by calling attention to its manifestations, possibly explaining its origins, and reassurances as to the analyst's nonjudgmental attitude. The interpretative process uses as evidence dreams, symbols, parapraxes, resistances, transference feelings of love that manifest neurotic preconditions for love, transference feelings of defiance of authority, and conflicts over perverse and inverse sexual desires.

It is not possible to overestimate the significance of this set of propositions concerning factors that induce emotional suffering and undermine adaptive mental functioning. Nothing in this chapter is intended to imply otherwise. The bulk of Freud's momentous contributions have remained fundamental to clinical work up to this day. Nevertheless, when viewed from today's vantage point, the good old days of interpreting sex are not all they seem to be. Analysts cannot in good conscience look back at those times comfortably. For one thing, it can be argued with confidence that early analytic work was replete with both self-misunderstanding and idealization. For another thing, the work did scant analytic justice to troubled analysands in that it yielded only simplistic, often misleading and implicitly moralistic idea of both the trials and tribulations of human development and existence and the joys and triumphs of life in a world of other people. Additionally, it is evident from all the changes that have taken place since that time that the early epistemology, methodology, and conceptions of interpretation and therapeutics, although pervaded by signs of genius, have not stood the test of clinical experience.

There is a cartoon that shows a choice point in the road, one sign pointing in the direction of unanswered questions and the other pointing in the direction of unquestioned answers. Today as never before is a time of questioning our analytic answers about sex. We have fewer unchallenged certainties to guide us, and we must tolerate greater ambiguity and controversy. Now, when we are presented in the clinical situation with sex, whether blatantly or only suggestively, we try as best we can to answer a host of questions, and often we come up short—and for most of us there is fortunately more tolerance for coming up short. Psychoanalysis has evolved into a slower, longer, and sounder process.

Among the questions being asked are these: Are we to take the sexual material for what it seems to be or must we suspend judgment and remain quietly observant for a while longer, perhaps an extended while longer? Then, once we have a sense of the material, should we address it explicitly, and if so, how and when, or should we contain our ideas and wait to express them at a time more propitious than the present one? What is a more propitious time? How best to prepare the way for it?

Additionally, is the talk of sex an evasion or disguise of hostility? Could it be a defensive retreat from a budding sense of dependency? Maybe it is a defensive show of pseudo-maturity or denial of gay or lesbian feelings through dramatized heterosexual behavior. And if it is gay or lesbian in appearance, could that be a denial of heterosexual feeling or could it be instead an achieved openness that manifests newfound confidence in the self, the analyst, and their relationship? Can we be sure it is not preoedipal sex? Is it possible that it is primarily a disguised form of preoedipal sex? Is it a power play—sadistic or masochistic—to gain control of the analyst through his or her countertransference? Is the sex, such as it is, ego-syntonic? A desperate attempt to prove that one is not feeling psychically dead or empty? Compliance with a real or imagined wish of the analyst?

Fundamentally, these questions are not new. In his many *clinical* discussions of sex, Freud made it clear that analysts must entertain all these questions and possibilities and more. When theo-rizing, however, he and others after him usually wrote about interpretation as though they could tell with certainty what was what and how to deal with it—too much so, it must now be said. They left clinical work encumbered with many unquestioned answers.

Today's analysts do not try to settle each problem straightaway as though going down an exhaustive or exhausting checklist; rather, they store these questions in preconscious contexts from which to draw when interpreting sex. Often they defer formulating questions altogether, recognizing that it can be more useful to wait until more is known and ambiguities have been reduced. Also, they are better prepared emotionally and intellectually either to revise conjectures and interpretations in the light of continuing dialogue with the analysand or to simply go on listening. (Not so simple in practice!) They do not "go by the book" and interpret mechanically or by formula; nor can they "go back to Freud," for there is no way to avoid the looming questions: Which book is that? Which Freud? Early Freud or later Freud? Melanie Klein's Freud, Hartmann's Freud, or Lacan's Freud? And so on.

Epistemologically, contemporary psychoanalysts have been moving away from Freud's frequent claims of pure scientific empiricism and inductive reasoning. Throughout this book and others (1976, 1983, 1992, 1997a), I have already discussed this shift at length. It is a shift away from such basic ideas that psychoanalysis cannot do without contingency-free essences that allow universalized propositions ("*the* libido," "*the* nuclear conflict of the neuroses") and the usefulness of grand polarities and binary divisions of major variables ("masculinity-femininity," "activity-passivity," "Life and Death Instincts"). Analysts have also been abandoning the position in which they take for granted the regular achievement of an objectivity totally free from value-laden emotional countertransferences, personal factors that, at least up to a point, slant their perceptions and conceptualizations.

What have we been moving toward? To summarize: we tend more and more to think in terms of constructivism, narration, dialogue, co-authorship, and a view of objectivity that exposes it as a rough consensual matter that is applicable only on a general level, only within a specific theoretical perspective, and situated in a cultural, ideological, historical context. Live experience is more likely to be worked through in terms of countertransference as well as transference. Being less threatened by diversity, we challenge normative propositions about sexual development and practice, about the primacy of sex in early development as against attachment and aggression, and about the primary importance of detailed reconstruction of infantile sex in the analytic process, especially in the interpretation of transference. By expanding the horizons of psychoanalysis in these ways, we insure its health while not turning our back on the past—though we do, as mentioned, reconceptualize it in different ways.

These changes steadily confront analysts with the question of what counts as evidence (see Schafer 1996). This question insinuates itself into many of our discussions in journals, meetings, and clinical conferences. Consequently, the ideal of establishing one final, incontestable set of truths about sex is fading as room is made for multiple truths that are not subject to one final integration. Every theory of sex is now contestable (Is sex the basic drive?) and reversible (Is sex a derivative of primary object relations?). The truths (in its terms) the theory leads to are always provisional and ultimately optional.

I argued in Chapter 1, "Insight into Insight," that the evidential value of the analysand's response to interpretation has been enhanced well beyond what Freud chose to emphasize. He helped analysts cope with the ambiguity of the analysand's accepting or rejecting an interpretation. Particularly important now is the analysand's subjective experience of being at the receiving end of a particular interpretation or of any interpretation at all. However, it may be a long time before latent experience can be defined and then only up to a point. We may, for example, come to understand that an interpretation of sex has been experienced at one time as a blow, at another as a moral judgment, a reassurance, a seductive move, a rape, or an insult. Thus, what is registered or heard may not correspond to the conventional sense of the analyst's action or his or her words. Moreover, there may be a countertransferential gap between what the analyst consciously intended and what the analyst conveyed, as, for instance, when an interpretation of an implied hostile feeling in a sexualized transference is conveyed with so much tentativeness or anxiety that it may well be warranted to say that the analyst is conveying fear of the analysand's aggression or fragility, and in either respect sending a message different from that consciously intended.

We know that interpretations can be formulated on various levels of mental functioning. Analysands in the paranoid-schizoid position respond better to interventions conceived in concrete terms that do not call for significant shifts to a reflective level, while those at or near the depressive position can entertain reflective comments provided that they are not too threatening. Also, the former will often talk in genital terms though their unconscious fantasies are likely to be expressed in oral and anal words and imagery with strong connotations of struggles with dependency, sado-masochism, omnipotence, and persecutory anxiety. Issues of reciprocity, mutuality, and self-critical reality testing will not mean much to them as they engage busily in their splitting, projective identifications, idealizations, and denials in their efforts to maintain psychic equilibrium. Often, it will be only through trial and error that the analyst will recognize the level on which the analysand can understand and perhaps be receptive to comments bearing on sexuality.

## CLINICAL EXAMPLES

*First clinical example.* Felix presented with a problem of premature ejaculations in his sexual affair with a sexually forward married woman. In the analytic sessions, his manner was charming, intelligent, consistently unruffled. In giving history, he spoke fondly of his mother and criticized his father as distant and competitive. Already, one might think of Freud's having proposed, in his "Contributions to the Psychology of Love" (1914), that impotence expresses the effects of unconscious oedipal conflict. In fact, Felix's analyst, a female supervisee, did soon comment in a way that pointed toward an oedipal interpretation. Soon afterwards, the sexual symptom disappeared. One might be tempted to conclude that the symptom's disappearance validated the oedipally slanted interpretation. Indeed, in the old days, some analysts might have predicted this result. But what if the analyst's comment was frightening enough to stimulate the flight into health that Freud always considered a possibility? Unconsciously, the analysand might have experienced it as the analyst's "coming" too soon. In fact, it was not long before Felix lost interest in the married woman and reverted to the relatively asocial lifestyle with which he had entered analysis. Once again, he seemed indifferent to sex. This sequence is not unfamiliar in clinical practice. Symptoms come and go for many reasons other than insightful working through.

A classical but more cautious Freudian analyst might infer from this clinical sequence of events only that the intervention was ill timed in that the ground had not been prepared for it, as, for example, it might have been had the analyst first brought it slowly into the transference. Then it might have turned out that the analysand's heterosexual movement had been in the service of his flight from an erotic transference to his female analyst and a bid for her affection by being a "good boy." That the change was not sustained might then testify only to the unanalyzed oedipal aggression in the transference along with continuing castration anxiety. All told, we could be contemplating an instance of what long ago Edward Glover (1931) would have subsumed under "the therapeutic effect of inexact interpretation."

I have presented this incomplete sketch of an extended line of oedipal thinking not as a correct set of conclusions, but rather as one way of inferring the level on which to interpret. However, the gist of a phallic-oedipal interpretation might have eluded Felix, because he was not amenable to interpretations formulated in a way that is appropriate to a basically objected-related person with an adequate capacity to think symbolically. Another analyst, focused on Felix's asocial lifestyle, might have reservations about this classical set of inferences and propose instead that Felix was living for the most part on the relatively more primitive paranoid-schizoid level of function. Then, Felix would be considered someone who is not strongly related to already differentiated objects through a reasonably defined self. This analyst would wonder if Felix might be a man afraid to abandon a mistrustful, narcissistic position. He or she might infer that Felix had merely yielded passively, partially, and briefly to the approaches of a seductive woman. Felix's transient sexual entanglement and symptoms might then be seen as also serving as a false front that had been unsuccessfully covering up a relatively unrelated mode of existence. That fragile front would have been buttressed by his social manner of impervious agreeableness— a not unusual clinical picture. Additional support for these inferences would be found in the obviousness of the initial suggestions of oedipal entanglement in that they seem served up on a silver platter. That obviousness can be a warning to look further before coming to conclusions about basic emotional dynamics.

What did Felix's subsequent treatment have to say about these alternative expectations? He replaced his initial complaint of sexual impotence with concern over his difficulty in forming relationships in general. In his transference, as elsewhere, he showed a powerful aversion to dependency. His manner remained controlled to such an extent that, taken together with his antidependency, it suggested unconscious fantasies of omnipotence as well as fear of the emotions inevitably stirred up in genuine relations with others, At one point, for example, when his attention was called to his rapidly suppressing an incipient expression of irritation with his analyst, he was equally quick to generalize the issue to "everybody" as in "that's how everybody is." He dealt with indications of mistrust in the transference in the same way. In this defensively impersonalized context, it began to seem that the inferred omnipotence had more to do with issues of maintaining control and unrelatedness than with classical oedipal variables.

This provisional formulation does not, however, rule out the role of oedipal variables in Felix's disturbance, for these variables are likely to have played some part in the choice of symptom. Interpretively, however, Felix came to be seen more and more as someone unable, at the time of the oedipal interpretation, to use higher-level interpretations. He had been too busy blocking incorporation of any and every interpretation in his efforts to ward off a sense of relatedness or dependency in the transference. The analyst learned to proceed slowly, to be far less ambitious in making interpretations while waiting to build trust and receptivity in other ways until Felix had inched his way up to the level where he would at times be capable of the symbolic functioning, presupposed by standard forms of interpretation. For a long time, the analyst had to demonstrate only an interest in getting to understand Felix, one that was not heavily freighted with conspicuous empathy or painful understanding.

When interpreting sex with an eye to available levels of functioning, one is not in an either/or position. Many analysands are continuously fluctuating in level in line with their histories, anxieties, and defenses. Nor is one obliged to take sides in theoretical debates about what the *real* issues are. It is all real, and to some degree it all pertains to sex. It is just a matter of not being so controlled by manifest sexual content that one uses it straightaway as the framework for interpretation. Being too focused on manifest content is exactly the wrong way to bring about analytically intelligible psychic change. Strengthening the foundations of relatedness to others may be required—most often it is required—before interpreting sex, in any useful sense of the term, can play a constructive role in the analysis.

*Second example.* Tim was not altogether different from Felix, though was able to be more reflective. He began one session reporting encouraging signs of decreased influence in his work of the fears and inhibitions that had been severely limiting his assertiveness and advancement. Almost immediately thereafter, however, he began seriously questioning whether analysis was doing anything for him. When I expressed interest in this turnabout, he reverted to familiar complaints about himself to the effect that he was a coward. The next day, he said he disliked my mentioning his changes for the better, because he felt that I was reassuring and protecting him. My doing so only made him feel diminished as a person. In conclusion, he said, reflectively, "I just don't want to receive."

Tim then reviewed his way of putting me into one of two roles: on the one hand, a harsh judge whose seemingly neutral or mildly empathic observations were veiled criticisms, demands, or instructions as to how he should have behaved and, on the other hand, a supportive figure who nevertheless demeans him even when only repeating what Tim himself has just mentioned as an achievement. When—perhaps prematurely—I then commented and explained that I considered both views of me to be expressing his anxiety-driven need to control me one way or another, he felt criticized. Throughout his remarks, guilt feelings were conspicuous by their absence.

Although I believe that many analysts would agree that Tim was relying on projection to wall himself off from me, I do not think they would agree among themselves why he was doing so or what he was trying to exclude. What did I stand for? What did my interventions stand for? Was he emotionally unprepared for understanding and being understood, in the manner described by Betty Joseph (1983) and elaborated in Chapter 1? In that case, he would have been appropriately warding me off. Was he avoiding the conflict between envy and gratitude, specifically envy of my goodness, sanity, and resoluteness? Did he conceive of gratitude as the first treacherous step to abject dependence? Yes would be the answer to these questions if one had first foregrounded the apparently reliable information that, from an early age and in response to two narcissistic, self-absorbed, unsupportive parents, one hypercritical and always mistrustful and the other an untrustworthy poseur, Tim had tried hard to be independent of others by always knowing better than they. Only in that way could he feel superior, if not secretly omnipotent, and justify his own lack of trust and his antidependency stance.

On the other hand, if one took into account Tim's equally long history of idealizing and adopting a macho mode of being, prowling for heterosexual conquests of women in whom he could not subsequently sustain interest, meanwhile feeling himself a coward, and also factored in the absence of a strong and reliable father figure in his life, then one might suspect that Tim was in the grip of an unconscious fear of homosexuality. This conjecture is consistent with the impression Tim gave that it was his father who was the warm parent while his mother was the hypercritical one. Tim might well have been unconsciously afraid that, defensively, he had over-identified with his mother and become feminine in relation to his father. Being macho would then have been his secondary defense, and being omnipotent and sexually predatory would be his way of reassuring himself against feelings of castratedness. Within this interpretive context, it could be supposed that Tim was experiencing my noting signs of progress as my way of being seductively exciting. Not that he was not leading me on by bringing up that kind of material. One could conjecture that for him, giving signs of dependency and trust were ambivalently regarded signs of femininity and stepping onto the slippery slope to homosexual love.

For what it is worth, reflecting on my own emotional stance, I could not make out any reactions one way or another to his news of beneficial change and its repudiation. As far as I could make out, I was neutrally intent on articulating the constituents of his obvious conflict. I did not see myself as stimulating his transference fantasy. Nor did I see myself in an either/or situation of interpretation. There was a lot of sexuality to interpret, but I believed there was no immediate call for me to bring up his experiencing my interventions as castrating penetrations. It seemed more to the point to explore how he took them as attempts to intrude on his omnipotence and to lure him into a needful, object-related state. Thus, I decided that what Tim required first and for a long time was some working through of his narcissistic disturbance: his hostile, controlling, omnipotent, paranoid transference that necessitated his blocked incorporation of what I had to offer. We had to reach a point where, with some degree of stability, he could enter into an analytic dialogue with me and not just talk at me or against me. Annie Reich's (1954) emphasis on the primitive foundations of a pathologically grandiose ego ideal seems more immediately applicable to Tim's makeup than standard discussions of higher-level phallic-oedipal conflicts. Tim was not yet ready for analysis of those issues, though he could intellectualize about them.

*Examples 3 and 4* are shorter. Both deal with women who presented prominent, though different, sexual problems, and both presented the analyst with the problem of finding the most useful level for effective clinical intervention. As with Felix and Tim, my brief accounts will not cover all the angles or resolve all the ambiguities. What follows merely illustrates a way of thinking about sexual material that does not rely relatively automatically on the many unquestioned answers about the primacy of heterosexuality that are strewn about our field of investigation—rote responses that everyone denies making and yet can be found in obvious or barely disguised form in many clinical reports.

Gina, my third example, was a young unmarried woman who presented as a severely repressed, timorous, submissive woman who had been crushed by an envious, vain, domineering, narcissistic mother and an indifferent but at times somewhat seductive father. Her sex life was quite inhibited; indeed, her relationship to, or use of, any of her bodily senses was strikingly limited. Initially, she gave no signs of responsiveness to any interventions touching on her desires, feelings, fears, or fantasies in the transference. So far as she could control things or acknowledge subjective experience, nothing was to pertain to excitement, sex, or romantic love. Clearly, it seemed, a clinical picture of significant sexual repression. Gina seemed to be leaving the field of sexuality to her vain mother while feeling hopeless about forming a gratifying bond with her father that was not frighteningly overexciting. These issues were dealt with later on.

The immediate issues in Gina's analysis seemed to be profound shame rather than guilt, enviousness, and, through projective identification, exaggerated fear of the envy of others; reactions against her deeply buried hostility, and feelings of superiority based on an identification with her mother that she obscured in the transference by meekly idealizing me. For a long time, these pressing features had combined effectively to render Gina almost totally impervious to analytic intervention. They were more than a first, rigid line of defense. It seemed that she had lived most of her life within the confines of a psychic retreat that provided secret sadomasochistic gratifications as well as defensive protection. At best, she had taken some tentative steps toward higher levels of function and had remained ready to regress from them at a moment's notice.

My *final example*, Diana, a young woman, presented a different picture. She was quite sexually active and usually involved with more than one man. Usually, she chose an older man; in this way seeming to be splitting her feelings into tender love and lustfulness. In both respects, it could be inferred that she was repetitively acting out the oedipal fulfillment of a childhood romance with her father who, by all accounts, was extremely overinvolved with her. Her life pattern seemed well suited to exclude experienced erotic feelings and desires in her transference. Diana's acting out had a desperate quality. She hoped analysis would help her feel more sure of herself, less ashamed, and better organized in her relationships.

Slowly, her analysis began to feature a deep sense of deadness and confusion based on major experiences of object loss and deprivation in early childhood. She was constantly warding off this sense of deadness by preoccupying herself with sexual fantasies and activity and with the apparently guilt-free, unconsciously oedipal gratifications she could obtain thereby. In the end, it even seemed that she had been leaving the analyst in the clear not just defensively but also to protect her chances to come back to life on this deeper level. Diana had turned to analysis not so much to resolve her sexual dilemmas, as to find a way of not feeling desperate about the threat of lifelessness deep within her. It was only much later that heterosexual and homosexual Oedipal themes in the transference and in her past life became available for effective analytic work, although they had come up from time to time earlier in the analytic process. Then, it was not yet timely to deal with them. Mostly it was her dread of her most regressive experiences that had to be expressed in her sessions and, so far as possible, mitigated. A mature oedipal-level, object related mode of being, which depends on developing toward or into the depressive position, could be taken up only later in the analysis when Diana was able to persist in being alive during times of stress.

## CONCLUDING REMARKS

Manifest references to sex issue from varied levels of psychic function, and they play different parts in the analyst's interpretive construction of the here-and-now analytic relationship. Once explored psychoanalytically, with special reference to transference and countertransference, that manifest material often leads into the unconscious fantasies characteristic of the paranoid-schizoid position, as described by Kleinian analysts. When this is so, alleviation of problems requires the analyst to work through many issues on the relatively narcissistic level that characterizes that psychical position.

# Psychoanalytic Discourse on Male Nonnormative Sexuality and Perversion

For some time, well-established propositions and forms of argument in the humanities and social sciences have been undergoing critical reappraisal. Strong arguments have been advanced against much of this received wisdom. It is said to be replete with unacknowledged ideological precommitments, cultural narrowness, ahistorical perspectives, unsupported conclusions, and self-contradiction. Meanwhile, pluralistic arguments and anti-foundational arguments have been gaining in persuasiveness and acceptance.

In many instances, feminists have been showing that pervasive prejudice against women, based on the kind of thinking that is now in serious question, has insinuated itself into the canon in each of these fields of study. As part of this project, they have shown that, in many instances, the traditional and universalized psychoanalytic conceptions of normal and pathological development have been biased in favor of men. As discussed in the preceding chapter, these conceptions sometimes tacitly and sometimes openly endorse conventional ideas of masculinity and femininity organized around re-productive sexuality. Thus, in this major area of human desire, con-flict, and forms of human relatedness, not all psychoanalysts have consistently lived up to their ideals of sustained curiosity and open-mindedness. Instead, some or many have mistakenly regarded moral value judgments as facts of nature, objective findings, or inevitable assumptions and conclusions. For them, one is supposed to receive all their prejudiced assertions as though being the beneficiary of sound reality testing, rational inference, and biological sophistication.

Phallocentrism in psychoanalysis has already been discussed at length from within psychoanalysis. I have made a few contributions to this literature (1974, 1978, 1992, 1994, 2001). A comparable upsurge has been taking place in the area of gay and lesbian studies (Abelove et al. 1993, Dominici and Lesser 1995). Here, I try to add something to existing studies of the psychoanalytic conceptuali-zation of male homosexuality. Then, in an effort to strengthen my argument, I develop a correlated and much-needed critique of the concept of perversion. I focus first on the way sexual and gender prejudices often rest on confusions between norms and moral val-ues, after which, with special reference to binary conceptualiza-tions, I take up the inimical influence of dichotomous or polarized thinking in the realm of sex and gender.

## NORMS AND MORAL VALUES

In his monograph *Psychoanalysis and Moral Values* (1960), Heinz Hartmann emphasized veiled moralizing. He pointed out that, in the course of child-rearing, when parents and educators think they are simply conveying facts about things and practices and thus are being merely descriptive, they are likely to be convey-ing moral preferences or imperatives; at least, so they are under-stood by their children and young students. It can be said that it is very much that way in the case of gender development. For, when the boy is told, "Boys and men do this, not that," "Boys are this way, not that way," "Boys aspire to this, not that," "Boys look good this way, not that way," and so on, he senses moral pressures in these factual statements. This we find to have been the case later on in our clinical analyses of adults, particularly in their struggles against certain thoughts, feelings, and desires in their transferences (see, for example, my essay, "Men Who Struggle against Sentimentality" [1992, pp. 116–127]). Similarly, "good for you," "bad for you," "the right way," "the wrong way," "nice," and "unpleasant," far from being intended and experienced merely as descriptive, can convey unstated moral preferences and imperatives and be so understood.

We enter here a major realm of object relations to which we were introduced psychoanalytically by Freud in "The Ego and the Id" (1923). There, he emphasized the child's identifying unconsciously with the parental unconscious superego. The boy's internalizing of moralistic traditions becomes the basis of his exerting the same influence when he is the parent of children, and so the process continues through the generations, whatever subsequent conscious modifications are introduced to suit the times. In clinical analysis, we find that, as children, our adult analysands regularly drew moral lessons from what was ostensibly realistic instruction about the conventions of the social world. The "facts" about being a boy imply to the boy that he will be loved, admired, and safe from persecutory responses if he conforms to the norm without question or protest. At the opposite extreme, he will be scorned, punished, and otherwise emotionally abandoned if he does not, and that is the way it frequently works out.

Going further, however, the boy develops extravagant notions in conscious and unconscious fantasy about the rewards and punishments that await him in either case. These imagined consequences—both exciting and terrifying—can and often do permanently affect his body, mind, or entire life. The rationalistic parents who, later on, say, "But we never threatened or preached; we only informed, and we always explained," do not recognize the influence of unconscious communication, fantasy, and internalization processes. Thus, communicating what is normative perpetuates the moral import and impact of conformity and nonconformity in the realm of sexuality and gender.

The superego identifications of childhood include more than self-condemnation. They include, as well, support for the defensive tendency to project what is felt to be undesirable or unsafe and to become persecutory toward those into whom one projects one's own forbidden, unspeakable, or unnameable desires. To some extent, the way is prepared for this mode of defense by parents, in their child-rearing practices, using projective identification of what they cannot accept in themselves. The child is assigned the burden of containing their unwanted, derogated, and feared selves.

Freud prepared us to recognize and interpret these abuses, derogations, ostracisms, and discriminations. He showed how polarization affects many crucial developmental and social aspects of human life, including our views of the lives of others. We understand how this paranoid drama is played out between men and women when men use women as the garbage cans for what they repudiate in themselves: desires for such "feminine" experiences as passivity, yielding, penetration, and motherliness. When they then go on to idealize what they have projected, they sharpen what they regard as *the* difference between the sexes, thereby deriving further reassurance and sense of integration with regard to their own gender identity. On this basis, we can understand a good deal about why homosexual proclivities and practices are ridiculed and otherwise persecuted by the majority of conventionally heterosexual boys and men.

In psychoanalysis, these redistributions of sexual tendencies cannot be regarded simply as the result of an inborn, biological ground plan. Whatever "nature" may contribute in this regard —and we should remain skeptical of any arguments based on simple biological determinism—it is clear that nurture within cultural settings, as elaborated in unconscious fantasy, plays a tremendous role in the development of these projectively developed, dichotomous splittings within the self and these persecutory attitudes.

## BINARY LANGUAGE AND VALUES

Transmissions of superego dictates concerning maleness occur in ways other than the use of projective and introjective communication of normative facts to children. A strong case can be made that the prime vehicle of transmission is language. Language appears to be structured to serve sexual and gender biases. Typically, its coercive power is not felt as such; rather, language is felt to be a transparent medium that enables clear perception and rational, adaptive instruction and action in the world of social relations. No doubt, it does enable organized thought and all the rest; however, it is also a medium so laden with moral messages that it regulates major aspects of our relations with ourselves, others, and events and things in the surrounding world. More than being enabling, language also exerts moral control over what is enabled.

For instance, ideas of facticity and objectivity are directed and shaped by the words we use and how we use them. In learning language, we take it for granted that words refer to fixed realities. Binary divisions stand out as seemingly unquestionable ways that things exist in nature. As a result, we often say "it" when all we can rightly say is that we are speaking from one possible perspective; we do not say "As I see it," or some equivalently perspectival utterance. This reliance on "it" gives that "it" moral weight, as though we are being not only correct but "good" in being correct about "it." Like "it," binaries serve as organizers of the welter of information and impressions with which consciousness is flooded by our inner and outer worlds. We grow up blind to the way we receive constructions of nature, and we add our own constructions as we go along. We do not recognize the extent to which we realize only some of the possible versions of whatever "nature" might become for us. Anthropological research shows this to be so.

Binary terms pervade our thinking about identity formation and/in human relationships. Psychoanalytic discourse contains its full share of polarities that seem to reflect nature. Masculine-feminine, heterosexual-homosexual, oedipal-preoedipal, genital-pregenital, paternal-maternal, active-passive: none of them irreducible factual observations; all of them organizing concepts. Unthinkingly, we come to understand these terms as referring to natural and complete opposites; perhaps amenable to being juxtaposed or included in an aggregate, but certainly—so we assume—their substructures are neither vague nor overlapping. Hence, "the opposite sex" and, in the usual absolute sense, "the difference between the sexes." It is only upon reflection, however, that we realize that they are merely established versions of "nature" and not the only ones possible.

Contemporary critical theory has also brought out how these imposed polarizations implicitly set up hierarchies of value. Typically, they favor attributing a higher value to the first term of the two (masculine, active, and so on). Also, as already indicated, this structural feature of language leaves no room for overlap and gradations; it is as though the second term is the weak tag-along. The dichotomous wording is understood to refer to clear-cut, symmetrical, but equally valued units of nature.

To a large extent, Freud placed this polarizing, valorizing, and simplifying mode of thought at the center of his theorizing. In contrast, in his clinical thinking, Freud was not severely constrained by dichotomization. In most of his clinical works he developed mixed and asymmetrical analyses. Often he subsumed these complex clinical accounts under the heading of overdetermination, and, as an advocate of scientific psychoanalysis and not realizing, as we can today, that narration is an aspect of all communication, he also regretted that these accounts were novelistic. Of Freud, we may say that he wrote at cross-purposes with himself, on the one hand universalizing, generalizing, and dichotomizing, and, on the other, impressively individualizing his analysands in his clinical presentations.

Our own clinical work follows Freud in these respects in that, as I understand it, we would all agree that we are constantly busy with mixed cases and questions of degree, and that, both clinically and professionally, much depends on the narrative skill with which we communicate our clinical work. We mistrust presentations based on totally balanced, black-and-white contrasts.

In theory construction, however, the binary problem remains with us, for the constituents of the mixtures continue to be regarded as symmetrical opposites (for example, object love and narcissism). Also, hierarchic valorizations within the binaries have not been eliminated. Theory construction is the operation that most plainly exposes the way in which basic constituents of language have continued to control the formulation of numerous psychoanalytic principles just as they shaped Freud's foundational works. Perhaps the problem shows itself most plainly in the realm of sexuality. Discussions of homosexuality show this to be so.

As people develop in their cultural setting, always limited by the simplistic modes of primitive thinking and built-in valorizations of polarized language, they approached the ideas of "the paternal" or "the maternal" and "the masculine" and "the feminine" as symmetrical opposites and as somehow implying differences in value. In the same way, people in general tend in their thinking, though less so in their sexual practices, to divide male and female bodies or genitals in this polarized way, as in the case of the erect penis and the female genitalia conceived as a hole to receive it: not just *a* hole; it is *the only* hole (the cloacal fantasy). Historical research has shown that, prior to modern times, anatomists considered this female "hole" the penis turned inside out (Laquer 1989).

Much of my evolution as a clinician and theorist has consisted of trying to divest myself as much as I can of psychoanalytically endorsed ideas of "opposites." "Opposites" were in play during my personal development and my clinical training. Some are still in play in our discipline, just as they are in Western culture. For some time now, like many other analysts, I have been trying to focus my clinical attention on the ways in which my analysands' thoughts are bound and blocked by dichotomous conceptions of the world and the self. Often enough, it turns out that when they seem to be using simple linguistic conventions, they are also giving signs that, unconsciously, they are controlled by powerful, black-and-white moral biases based on superego-enforced projections, introjections, and idealizations. Analytically, we understand these features to be associated with infantile anxiety, guilt, envy, and persecutory orientations.

At our analytic best, we focus on differences, not opposites. Difference, too, is a selectively organizing concept in that, arbitrarily, it can overlook much resemblance or identity; such is the case, for example, in thinking about men and women. Nevertheless, the idea of difference still leaves far more room than "opposites" for the analytic ideals of open-mindedness and curiosity. On balance, "difference" encourages us to individualize our analytic interpretations, and it pushes aside grand classifications, developmental ground plans, and diagnoses. Thinking along these lines in connection with anthropological fieldwork, the noted methodologist Clifford Geertz recommended aiming for "thick description" of single scenes, events, and persons (1973).

As well as divesting myself as much as I can of binary classifications, I have developed a tentative, if not suspicious, attitude toward all universalizing propositions about men, women, fathers, mothers, sons, daughters, child-rearing practices, and psychosexual development. I think the key issues of psychoanalysis have been saddled with over-ambitious and unwarranted generalizations. In response to the anxiety-inducing aspects of our work, we have been using these sometimes helpful but often disruptively reductive classifications and diagnoses more than we should. Our doing so is inimical to the analytic attitude of empathic listening and graphic description. Too often, these generalizations are based on questionable dichotomizations and arbitrary symmetrical descriptions. Also, they promote ever-new ways of interfering with individualized analytic thinking. As a result, the writings of many analysts seem repetitious, formulaic, and uninformative.

These remarks about individualization are not intended to argue that some pure phenomenology exists that is sacrificed in the process of generalizing. Phenomenology, too, is selective, being always shaped by existing conceptual and narrative commitments (Schafer 1992). "Thick description" that serves individualization and the specification of differences is necessarily guided by conceptual conventions. What is being argued here is that in the realm of sexuality and gender, implicitly moralized binary thinking supports biased thinking.

## MALE NONNORMATIVE SEXUALITY

I turn now from this general scrutiny of psychoanalytic discourse and the place in it of unhelpful, value-laden dichotomies and generalizations to the topic of male nonnormative sexuality: the sexual desires for, fantasies about, and practices of men with men that are considered by many to be "altogether different" at best and "bad" or "evil" at worst. As I mentioned, it is particularly the nonconformist practices that threaten those who are polarized by binary thinking and who, on this basis, have become fierce advocates of whatever they believe is normative. Polarized men need to buttress their own identities by surrounding themselves in fact or fiction with "real men" and "real women," and to regard "others" as objectionable, dangerous, and even punishable.

Binary thinking naturalizes cultural and historical differences. These differences are made to seem no more than stable facts of nature, as I mentioned. Once naturalized, any quality or process will be taken as simply human and inevitable, and the idea that people are following norms and defending them vigorously need not be taken into account. Ironically, one of Freud's (1907, 1908) greatest contributions was his denaturalizing prevailing convictions about the sexual innocence of children and related convictions about the affects of disgust, shame, fear, and guilt. However, and regrettably, he also valorized the idea of a heterosexual, genital, reproductive culmination of development. He could not go all the way with the curiosity that led to his being able to denaturalize as much as he did in the realm of sexuality, which was plenty.

Although Freud's conscious orientation to sexual variation does not seem to be at all condemning or persecutory, he stopped being tirelessly analytic when confronted with men's nonnormative sexuality. He generalized that all nonnormative forms of sexuality are signs of arrested development, that is to say, they indicate that the subject has been held up at one of the pregenital way stations to reproductive heterosexuality (see Freud 1922). Thus, nonnormative becomes a special form of disturbed development. Ostensibly nonjudgmental, this conclusion reaffirmed the morality of Freud's time, in what can be regarded as a pseudoscientific, hastily biologized way. For, unconsciously, there is no impermeable line between the idea that there is something different about you and something wrong with you; nor is there that line between psychologically wrong and morally wrong. That is one major reason why, to take a common clinical instance, most children and grown-ups tend to feel humiliated and vulnerable by admitting publicly that they are seeing a "shrink."

All the more so is this case when it comes to gay proclivities. Today, many gay men have adopted a militant stance with regard to this moral pressure exerted by so many in their worlds; yet I think it is safe to say that most people continue to regard every gay and "perverse" tendency as a stigma or sin against God or "nature." Comparatively few remain aware of mixed cases and degrees of one tendency mixed with the other.

What Freud did in the realm of sexual orientation and practices was to mistake a norm as a fact of nature. How he came to reach this wrong conclusion in the realm of sexual orientation, object choice, and practices, and what was entailed by that conclusion, I first took up in my initial contribution to this topic, "Problems in Freud's Psychology of Women" (1974), and I touched on it briefly in Chapter 6. In brief summary, I maintained (and I still maintain) that Freud's Darwinism led him to adopt an evolutionary ethic. In current terms, we might say instead that his conformist tendencies facilitated his using the Darwinism he valued as a scientist to support the evolutionary ethic. Viewing the individual as the carrier of the reproductive organs and substances designed to guarantee the survival of the species, he reasoned that it was essential that there be successful transmission of the germ plasm from generation to generation. It followed that psychosexual development *should* culminate in genital, heterosexual, reproductive sexuality. Anything else goes against the plan of nature. While he was taking this teleological set of assumptions for granted, Freud was also contradicting himself by showing how many trials, tribulations, temptations, and deterrents the child encounters along the road to that "ideal" end point. He showed that there are many phases, modes, zones, pleasures, pains, and fantasies the boy must deal with along the way and that he can fixate on any one of them. And yet Freud continued to consider the procreative end point the only one that was complete and therefore "natural."

In this way Freud naturalized and implicitly moralized norma-tive sexual inclinations and practices. He seemed not to see that he was leaping from biological norms to moral judgments when he as-sumed that development *ought to* culminate in reproductivity. He did not see the moralistic bias in reasoning that, because develop-ment *can* and usually does proceed to reproductivity, it *should* do so. But does this reasoning prove that only the reproductive heterosexual man is mature, normal, healthy, fully developed in his psychosexual-ity—a better-off person and by implication (which, in the individual case, Freud consciously would have repudiated), a better sort of per-son—than others who have developed differently. Once Freud had idealized procreation in the conventional way, he had to see the other forms as immature, unfortunately arrested, perhaps irremedi-ably so, although under ideal circumstances they might be amenable to the growth-enhancing method of psychoanalysis. Thus, just as in his phallocentric way he regarded the clitoris as a stunted organ, he was regarding men who diverged from the procreative norm as stunted human beings.

Manifestly, Freud's stance was usually that of a strict empiri-cist. He had what he took to be sound, supporting, empirical evi-dence for these conclusions about sexuality. When he looked in depth at his sample of homosexual patients and saw much uncon-scious sexual conflict and exaggerated defense involving fear, envy, rivalry, resentment, feelings of damagedness, narcissistic excess, and so on and so forth, he had, it seems, found all the evidence he needed to clinch his argument. But that conclusion of his argument was already in his mind as we can see in his much earlier correspon-dence with Fliess (Freud 1954). The preconceptions and the value judgments were all there, poised to strike.

In fact, however, nothing conclusive follows from Freud's ob-servations of the troubles of homosexual and otherwise "perverse" patients. For one thing, a small sample of patients does not license

one to generalize about a large class of people. Also, many heterosexual analytic patients shows the same or similar conflicts, even
the same intensity of conflict and defense, and the same or similar
disturbing developmental circumstances. It was Freud himself who
opened our eyes widest to this state of affairs. Furthermore, he recognized that psychoanalysis does not yield up the necessary and suf-
ficient conditions to predict final outcomes of development. In his
sounder methodological moments, he pointed out that analytic explanation works much better retrospectively; that is to say, it pro-
vides a basis for postdiction, not prediction.

I believe that Freud used other observations to support his conclusions. For example, many heterosexually active, neurotic men
seemed to derive therapeutic benefits from the analysis of unconscious conflicts over gender identity and sexual object choice.
Again, it must be noted that, for several reasons, nothing conclusive
follows from these observations. For present purposes, I shall emphasize only one of these reasons. Freud's Darwinian ideology committed him to try to bring his heterosexual patients to more integrated, comfortable, gratifying, heterosexual reproductive positions.
For their part, almost all his analysands were similarly committed.
Once analysis helped them to recognize that unconscious "perverse" and "inverse" tendencies were crucial components of their
pathogenic conflicts, they were eager to master them, if not get rid
of them. Relieved of the weight of these difficulties by analysis, and
helped toward a mixture of insight, renunciation, sublimation, and
continued repression, these men could hope to succeed in achieving
genital heterosexual love, reproductivity, and pleasure instead of suffering. They and Freud were together in this. It was not the kind of
togetherness that would have called attention to the considerable
amount of transference-countertransference collusion in which
they were engaged. Common cause has that blinding effect on clinical analytic work.

By and large, this common cause still seems to characterize
many analytic treatments. Many, if not most, analysts and analysands take heterosexual tendencies for granted. They agree that it
is specifically conflict over these tendencies that should be exam-

ined, understood, and reduced. For example, one can see how much this is the case by observing the regularity with which analysts who are describing gains in their case reports emphasize the factors of getting married and having children or at least moving in that direction. In contrast, homosexual and "perverse" tendencies, so often embedded in conflict, are considered central to psychological problems, and it is the temptation to act on them in fact or fantasy that is to be closely examined, understood, and so far as possible and reduced in the analysis, and then emphasized in clinical reports. Strong cross-gender identifications must be modified, pregenital fixations loosened so far as possible, and the troublesome non-normative tendencies finally subordinated to heterosexual genital primacy. Commonly, the analysand will accept a degree of latent homosexuality and perverse leaning as "natural" and to be expressed through foreplay, aim-inhibited friendships, empathy, and creativity—presumably, just as their analysts do. Basically, however, renunciation or diversion of some kind is the implied goal.

In this situation, there is little or no recognition of other lines of argument for example, that laid down by Judith Butler (1990). She showed how one could use Freud's own explanation of the passing of the Oedipus complex, in his monograph "The Ego and the Id" (1923), to draw conclusions that differ from Freud's. Specifically, she read Freud to be showing that identification with the lost oedipal object—the parent of the opposite sex—should favor a predominant identification with the opposite sex and thus promote normative homosexual resolutions of that complex. Although Freud noted this residual problem in his theory of psychosexual development, he did not deal with it effectively. He tended to fall back on ad hoc assumptions about constitutional differences and unspecified quantitative factors, and reproductive destiny.

## PERVERSION AND HOMOSEXUALITY

One aspect of Freud's idealization of normative heterosexuality is his characterizing the young child as "polymorphous perverse."

Under this heading he included the homoerotic or "inverse." Polymorphous, yes, but why perverse? To confront the pejorative implications of the term perversion, one need only turn to the *Shorter O.E.D.* (1973): "Perversion: . . . turning aside from truth or right; perversion to an improper use; corruption, distortion . . ." Furthermore, the history of the word perversion includes major legal and religious ideas of impropriety. Thus, there can be no question that "perversion" and "perverse" are loaded with moral connotations. Significantly, the *O.E.D.* uses a statement by Bacon as an illustrative quotation: "Women to govern men . . . slaves (to govern) free men . . . (are) total violations and perversions of the laws of nature and nations." The very choice of example naturalizes moral condemnation of those with feminist leanings along with non-normative sexuality. We may recognize the same bias in daily speech when "straight" is used for normative heterosexuality: straight as opposed to what—crooked, twisted, off the mark?

We ought to ask why Freud used the word "perverse" in a conventional way. After all, he was repositioning his readers to adopt many new and radical points of view on sexuality. Why did he seem to stop thinking creatively here and simply go along with conventional linguistic distinctions? What blocked the further reach of his curiosity? I contend that, in his theorizing, Freud was looking backward from the teleologically prescribed end point of Darwinian sexual development. Even his use of the word pregenital indicates this looking backward, for that "pre" implies that one is speaking of a normal future and thus of how the individual *ought to* get beyond inclinations of earlier times. It is implied that it is not enough to stay with such words as oral, anal, phallic-exhibitionistic, and dyadic. What is required is submission to the prescriptive use of the prefix "pre."

The word "preoedipal" is closely allied with the word "pregenital." Preoedipal, too, is a teleological, implicitly moralistic term. It naturalizes a conventional form of gender role development that, since Freud, has usually been understood in the sense of the "positive" (sic) oedipal. The "positive" oedipal is the crystallization, though not the culmination, of heterosexual development. Freud

regarded the "negative" oedipal, which he identified and emphasized especially in "The Ego and the Id," as the site of homosexual
love as well as the capacity to identify with "the opposite sex." Nevertheless, Freud tended to neglect the "negative" oedipal in many of
his formal theoretical writings. In the same way, he usually ne-
glected to go into detail about mothers in his patriarchically oriented case histories. And in his theories he usually situated this
woman in "positive" oedipal contexts; there, she remained the relatively unarticulated sex object of the "positive" oedipal boy and the
unarticulated rival of the "positive" oedipal girl. It seems justified to
conclude that the word *preoedipal* refers prescriptively to what is
preheterosexual as well as pregenital.

Freud's restricted and restricting use of "pre" indicates that he
stopped short of asking what he might have been expected to ask
had he continued to exercise his enormous curiosity. Specifically
with regard to castration anxiety, he did not ask, "What would there
have to be about the boy's development prior to this moment of
anxiety that would make him that vulnerable and impel him toward
all the painful choices and consequences traced out by psychoanalysis?" To ask this question, Freud would have had to acknowledge the
central and often disturbing role in development played by the early
child–mother relationship. In his later years, and presumably under
pressure from female colleagues, Freud did acknowledge the importance of that early relationship. However, that he did so with some
uncertainty and ambivalence can be inferred from his having reverted, in his very late paper on termination (1937) and in his
"Outline" (1939), to castration anxiety and penis envy as the
bedrocks. As such, they signify that the normal and proper outcome
of psychosexual development is reproductive heterosexuality to be
reached by way of a "positive" Oedipus.

Looking at the prefix "pre" in this light, as I believe we should,
there seems to be no reason to include it in discussions of the gratifications, frustrations, attachments, and fears characteristic of the
very first years of development. It is more consistently analytic to
take up these features of early development on their own terms, so
far as one can. Their subsequent transformations, if any, should not

intrude into the very beginning of discussion. That is the way of unhampered curiosity; any other way, by implying that these features are not yet the real thing, marginalizes them. Certainly, contemporary, analytically oriented developmental research and contemporary clinical practice restore these early features to a major place in developmental theory without in any way minimizing the importance of their later transformations, the transformations on which Freud centered so rewardingly.

In this perspective, we can expect it to be just as helpful when looking forward to use the term "post-dyadic" for the later development and, when looking backward, to speak of the preoedipal and pregenital. Only by looking in both temporal directions do we begin to limit the influence of value-laden teleological constraints. This bidirectionality throws into question the psychoanalytic use of "perverse" and "perversion."

It must be added that aesthetic value judgments and idealizations of the machine are often implied in the idea of reproductively oriented genital primacy. With regard to the aesthetic, Freud argued that normally oral, anal, and phallic exhibitionistic tendencies are subordinated to the heterosexual genital intercourse of adult sexual life. They are, he said, features suitable for foreplay. He implied then that, in that role, they might be pleasing without being indecorous. He also implied that it would go against the ideals of integration and maturity if, instead of repudiating or sublimating these tendencies, one were to linger too long over their direct gratification. Worse still, to be altogether gratified by them. He viewed their considerable sensuous and object-relational potential with great reserve. In an unobtrusive way, he added being decorously pleasing to the virtues of being stable, clear-cut, and continuing the species.

Idealization of the machine also flourished in the era of early Darwinian discourse. Both the powerful and efficient machine and the complex and intact organism were central to many metaphors and valorizations of his day. Often, they were, and they still are, metaphors for one another, as in the ideas "organic society" and the body as a "wonderful machine." The pressure is toward symmetrical conceptualization, unity, and efficiency: there should be no loose

ends, everything in its expected place, and no Oscar Wildes to contend with. Blurred boundaries, unpredictability, and conspicuous
deviance in the realm of sex: none of them pleasing or productive.

Thus did materialistic-utilitarian values seem to join with aesthetic values as vehicles for moral proscription and prescription in
the realm of sexuality and gender identity.

## CONCLUDING REMARKS

Freud may be viewed as having been working in conformity
with the moral, aesthetic, and material, and linguistic dictates of his
culture. His powerful use of the language of his time and his cultural
setting not only endorsed prevailing values, it loaded his discourse
with them. The idea of perversion is one manifestation of this
bias, and homosexuality as arrested development is another.
Today, we realize more than ever that language is far more than a
tool of thought or a transparent vehicle for the content of
thought. We realize that words teach us what to think, how to
think, how not to think, what to shun and persecute, and so how
to get along in society. They naturalize ideas that are merely versions of the world that befit their time and place, and by so doing
they lead us away from reflecting on that most urgent realm of
existence that we designate "sexual differences." Some prominent
aspects of these "differences" are central to gender jokes, as I will
try to show in the following chapter.

# 8

# Gender Jokes/Sexual Politics

Most of the innumerable jokes about relations between the sexes ("gender jokes" hereafter) may be approached interpretively as interventions in sexual politics. Far from being value-free, these tales take sides in conflicts over sexual prowess, power, competence, handicaps, and self-esteem. Additionally, these gender jokes may be said to endorse certain distributions of power and claims of integrity. They do so by tolerating or condemning violations of physical and ethical boundaries and by fostering proud, complacent, contemptuous, envious, and self-abasing attitudes. Frequently intermingled with the sexual/political interpretations to be developed here will be inferences bearing on other discriminatory attitudes based on social class, wealth, possessions, and ethnicity. In this chapter, I will detail numerous insights into gender jokes.

There are, of course, other jokes that tell the same kinds of stories about homoerotic and onanistic situations and practices. Although jokes of this sort will not be featured in what follows, I will sometimes note their nameless presence in some of the heterosexual stories.

My manifest focus will be narrow: negative stereotypes of women around which many gender jokes are organized—specifically, women as whores and women as avengers. At first and casual glance, these stories might appear to make a straightforward case for a one-dimensional and clear point of view on relations between men and women; however, when subjected to close analysis, they prove to be multidimensional, bearing on many aspects of heterosexual relationships and resonating on more than one level of psychic functioning.

My analyses will highlight themes of unconscious sexual and aggressive fantasies and the defenses against them, and where appropriate they will situate these themes, as mentioned, in the context of bias of different kinds. Problems in intergenerational relationships will also be teased out. In addition to the literal and symbolic content of the joke specimens to be discussed, I will also clarify the messages relayed by such structural aspects as silences, simplifications, blind spots, and innuendos.

In an earlier publication (1994, pp. 35–56), I included analyses of two sexual/political jokes. One joke concerns the general use of the pronoun "he" to refer to people in general. That traditional usage is also reflected in the view of God as male and of humanity as mankind. This usage implicitly leaves women in an objectified and genderless state. The other joke is a tale of men's locker-room braggadocio: in a conversation between two men, one of them in just three words—responding "Compared to whom?" when asked in a sociable way, "How's your wife?"—simultaneously boasts of sexual prowess, degrade women, and throws up a homophobic barrier. There, my analysis of these two jokes made up part of a general discussion of gendered discourse. Here, I will be concentrating on jokes, using for my purpose jokes of different sorts. Before moving on to these jokes, I will summarize the two contributions to the psychology of jokes—by Freud (1905b) and Ernst Kris (1938, 1940)—that lie at the foundation of the present discussion. As I proceed, I will supplement these contributions with some ideas of my own.

## NOTES ON THE PSYCHOANALYTIC
## PSYCHOLOGY OF JOKES

Freud's interest in jokes and the comic may be dated at least from the time he began to write on psychotherapy. It was not until 1905 that he published his famous monograph on jokes ("jokes" being Strachey's compromise term for the variety of comical narratives and events that Freud took up). Freud's interest seems to have been stimulated by frequent encounters with amusing verbal and linguistic twists in dreams, errors, and other clinical phenomena. He developed an understanding of jokes as unconsciously devised vehicles to express repressed wishes; being repressed, these wishes are taken to be caught up in conflict. Freud's understanding of these conflicts was paralleled and reinforced by his wide-ranging interest in myth, art, and other cultural phenomena. These, like jokes, seemed to express the same repressed wishes and defenses he was defining in his clinical practice.

Freud's theoretical and clinical understanding of jokes also included recognition that they are a necessary and inevitable part of social life. To be told successfully, they require a certain kind of actual or imagined audience. Consequently, in his endeavor to develop a general theory of the comic, he had to go beyond analyzing it in terms of both narrative structure and individual dynamic tensions. He had also to begin making a place in the psychology for psychosocial, relational variables, including seductiveness, differences in social class, ethnic background, and the conventions of male-female relationships. Regrettably, he did not carry these aspects of his joke psychology very far.

The next great psychoanalytic step forward was taken by Ernst Kris (1938, 1940). In his writings on the comic, he was reworking Freud's discoveries to bring them into line with Freud's 1923 tripartite (id-ego-superego) structural model and to develop the special relationship of jokes to Freud's (1926) second theory of anxiety. That theory centered on the real and imaginatively exaggerated danger situations of early childhood that are carried forward into the unconscious fantasies of adult life, and it defined anxiety as an affect signal given off by the ego when it recognizes danger. Specifically, Kris emphasized that the success of jokes seems to depend on their touching on danger situations and their associated conflicts that *the ego has not yet fully mastered*, though it has mastered them sufficiently to leave the jokes' audience feeling not acutely threatened. In his words, ". . . most comic phenomena seem to be bound up in past conflicts of the ego . . . They help it repeat its victory and in doing so once more to overcome half-assimilated fear" (1952, p. 215). Thus, the necessary conditions of a joke's success include a tolerable amount of anxiety, guilt, and shame. The listener is relieved by the joke's reduction of the implied unconscious dangers, as if saying, "See, there is not much to fear!" That relief of tension is then expressed in laughter.

On this basis, Kris explained why some jokes fail in general and some fail only with specific listeners. Those that fail in general either stimulate intense anxieties that are virtually universal, such as those occasioned in most people by suffering mutilation or perpetrating it, or else they have been told too ineptly or crudely to affect the hearer in the desired manner. In the case of individual failures, the joke may have been told to someone who, defensively, is in a precarious psychological position, that is, someone with so little sense of mastery of the implied unconscious conflicts and anxieties that he or she cannot enjoy fantasy or "childish" play or any of the other aspects of "letting go," a prerequisite of enjoying jokes. If not that, then the joke may have been told to someone with extremely rigid defenses against the specific libidinal or aggressive conflicts touched on by the narrative.

For example, when someone is not amused by gender jokes that are generally considered funny by persons who are situated in a similar social position, who hold similar values and share a similar cultural background, we may infer that the problem lies not in the quality of the jokes or joke-telling but rather in the listener's pressing conflicts and the kind of humorless social decorum or inhibition that she or he must insist on in order to maintain psychic equilibrium. It is commonly said of such people that they are too "uptight" or perhaps, in today's world, and often unjustly, "too politically correct."

I believe that the neo-Kleinian approach to gender jokes would have this to add to Freud's and Kris's contributions: first, that joke-telling depends on an implicit agreement to play out unconscious fantasies of omnipotence. Omnipotence comes into play through the joker's using the story to control the audience's fantasies and to expose them then to the surprise of the punch line and the semi-involuntary release of laughter. The audience may then be said to initiate not only the willing suspension of disbelief that is a prerequisite of emotional participation in artistic productions but also a willing suspension of knowingness, control, and decorum.

Secondly, the gender joker trades more or less openly on incompletely mastered narcissistic issues along with the phallic-genital-oedipal issues and the pregenital issues of the sort usually emphasized by Freud and Kris. These narcissistic issues include omnipotence-based struggles against dependency, the pressures of persecutory anxiety that result from splitting and projective identification of aggressive and self-abasing tendencies; also, envious and idealizing tendencies and denials, and coping with one's own ties to "bad" internal objects, ties that are primarily dyadic and centered on relations with maternal figures. For the most part, these narcissistic issues are subsumed under the paranoid-schizoid position (Klein 1946). This position is fluid, concretistic, and often tumultuous. In its primordial psychical reality, stable and secure loving relationships cannot be established or maintained.

In contrast to this position stands the depressive position (Klein 1940, Steiner 1993), a mode of fashioning a life that features creativity, a relatively stable predominance of integration and responsibility, and a readiness for relatively conflict-free and relatively anxiety-free loving relationships with others. Whatever the strengths it implies, the depressive position remains permanently vulnerable to some degree and duration of regression to the paranoid-schizoid. There is where one encounters the dramatized versions of women as whores and avengers.

## WOMAN AS WHORE

*First Joke.*

A young woman at a party is awestruck by the size and brilliance of the diamond in the ring on the finger of another, older woman whom she does not know. She rushes up to her and expresses her awe and also her curiosity. "Oh, yes," replies the older woman, "this is the Lipschitz diamond. It is gigantic, flawless, and priceless. The only trouble is, it comes with a curse." Surprised and fascinated, the young woman asks, "And what is the curse?" To which the older woman answers, "Lipschitz."

The obvious butt of this joke is the man Lipschitz; his accursed victim is the bejeweled woman. Implicitly, however, the joke is doubled in that it mocks her, too. This doubleness contributes to this gender joke's being interesting and effective; for it implies that the glittering woman has sold herself for ostentatious display of wealth. At least, she has been passively, masochistically acquiescent to a miserable relationship for the sake of material advantage. Living with the uncertainty and unhappiness often doled out to women in our society, many women do just what Mrs. Lipschitz did, and if we take into account how many men are in a similar situation at work and in allied situations, we can appreciate that the problem of accepting a miserable compromise for material advantage is not limited to women and that men have reasons of their own find the joke funny. Thus, along with mockery of women and attack on men's use of material advantage to exploit women we encounter in this joke a dimension of general pathos.

Considered in these terms, the joke emerges as more than a cynical narrative of brutish men buying and abusing women who, if the price is right, can be counted on to sell themselves into a masochistic existence. Additionally, it evokes some identification with the victims of power, money, social class, and perhaps their masochistic participation in victimhood as well. Thereby, the joke aims to elicit either lofty pity or compassionate empathy, or both. The end result will depend on the listener's identifications and defenses.

In yet another of its dimensions, this joke's dismal portrayal of materialistically shaped relations between the sexes corrupts the ostensibly spontaneous, awestruck young woman. For, with her eyes and her mind only on the diamond, she is portrayed as limited to bringing herself into relation to the object on display. The bejeweled woman becomes not much more than another object, a pedestal that holds the priceless treasure. Thus, the young woman depersonalizes the other woman and in so doing demeans herself. Simultaneously, she could be introducing the worm of envy into her superficial idealizing of the woman; for her gushy and crassly depersonalizing move strongly suggests a transference enactment based on projection of a powerful internal maternal figure. In this enactment, she turns the tables. In one stroke, she demolishes the object, thereby serving the interests of oedipal-triangular, and narcissistic-dyadic grievances, rivalries, and disillusionments.

An additional factor is brought to the fore by asking, "What about the joke-teller?" If the joke is being communicated just to get a laugh, the jokester is provisionally accepting and enjoying this dismal portrayal of relations between the sexes and between the generations of women as well. For the sake of a laugh, she or he temporarily adopts a manic posture in relation to this drama of power, possession, and masochism. Presenting the story as funny perpetrates a denial of both inflicting and suffering pain and humiliation. In this way it invites ego-syntonic distancing of oneself from yet another instance of the shared and often difficult state of affairs in the lives of many women and men.

Finally, the name Lipschitz introduces a derogatory view of Jews as crassly materialistic and sado-masochistically related to others. Mrs. Lipschitz herself is made out to be an embodiment of both "feminine" wiles and self-abasement. The joke may also cater to the self-mocking attitudes of many Jews, attitudes that usually simultaneously imply some identification with, and manic triumph over, those who aggress against them.

Applying the thesis advanced by Kris, one could say that those who laugh comfortably at this joke are the ones most likely to be relatively poised in these respects, that is, less rigid, troubled, cynical, or pathetic than those who are put off or fail to get the point. They are likely to exemplify adequately but still incompletely mastered conflicts in these realms of gender, power, psychosexual and psychosocial relations, and material, class, and ethnic values and biases. The same would be true of the effective joke-teller. All of them differ from those who, because they are intensely ideologically committed in one respect or another or for reasons of a painful sort, cannot enjoy the joke freely or at all.

In general, the pleasure gain made possible by the joke is that of a manic moment. Through denial of persisting conflict, the joke offers a temporary respite from what Freud called the miseries of everyday life.

*Second Joke.*

> There was a young woman from Kent
> Who said that she knew what men meant,
> When they asked her to dine,
> Gave her flowers and wine—
> She knew what they meant and she went.

This limerick obviously represents the woman as a bought woman. Like a whore, she is prepared to sell herself to men for what she gets out of them. However, the limerick also implies a triumph over men, for it is being suggested that, however much macho men may pride themselves on being sexually smooth and materially powerful seducers, they are nevertheless being used by the women they have targeted. The Kentish woman is only pretending to be seduced in a passively gratified state. Somewhere, G. B. Shaw put it this way: "A man pursues a woman until she catches him." Power is not always what it seems to be. By exploitatively defeating her men through pretended naïveté and compliance, the young woman of the joke is mocking stereotypical assertions of phallic, social, and material power, thereby scoring a victory in the socio-sexual wars between the sexes. Perhaps "trade-off" better describes these crosscurrents of exploitation.

The limerick may be understood as setting up a complex and ambiguous interplay of activity and passivity, assertiveness and submissiveness, strength and weakness, and seduction and exploitation. This interplay is definable not only in male-female relationships but in all social relationships. Because every one of these conventional polarities, no matter what their individualized elaborations, is likely to continue to remain an unsettled matter in the minds of men and women, the limerick has a good chance of entertaining members of both sexes, members of different generations, and all those who are alive to the ambiguities that pervade human relationships.

### Third Joke.

There is an aphorism that says, "If a lady says no, she means maybe; if she says maybe, she means yes; and if she says yes, she's no lady."

These lines are notable for excluding the possibility of a woman saying and meaning "no" in response to a sexual advance. They also exclude the possibility that a woman could say "yes" in reply or take the initiative herself with dignity and power of her own. The implied unconscious fantasy seems to be that any woman, regardless of her emphasis on propriety, is more or less readily and passively, perhaps weakly available to sexually predatory men. The joke suggests that the world of women can be considered equivalent to a man's harem, women varying merely to the extent that they play hard to get. Thus, it conveys the narcissistic, phallic fantasy in which women are more or less interchangeable and defenseless sex objects on the order of concubines. The macho man seems to prevail.

When viewing the aphorism this way, one can also appreciate that it enforces the conventional, double-standard idea of being "ladylike" with respect to sexual activity—an aspiration that also implies hopes to rise to a higher social class as imagined by those lower on the conventional social scale. Specifically, a lady should be devoid of sexual self-assertiveness, if not of desire itself. And while men do not have to be gentlemen, women do have to be "ladies"—in that oppressed, repressed, and self-denying sense of the term. That is the sense implied in the premarital sexual advice allegedly given to British upper-class young women: "Lie back and think of England."

Matters are, however, far more complicated than that. What must also be taken into account is that not all men accept the double standard eagerly or triumphantly. For some men, the very idea of enforcing brute phallic power continues to stimulate anxiety, guilt, or shame; this despite widespread and conspicuous changes in contemporary social mores. These men might enjoy this joke to the extent that it appeals to their longings to overcome inhibitions provided that they are not extreme.

The joke's complexity becomes plainer once we consider that this aphorism can also be understood as attributing to women a special kind of wiliness in relation to men. Specifically, men can't be sure what women mean, for they have their own desires and their own ways of going about gratifying them. Being ambiguous helps them exploit men by enforcing a social code that is very much to their advantage: while seeming to comply by adopting their masks of propriety, they retain and exercise power. This is another form of the wiliness displayed by the young woman from Kent.

The joke's doubleness, its portraying woman as both weak-minded and wily, may be thought to increase its comic impact on those who retain some, but not too much, cautious alertness to the subtly controlling ways of women while continuing to feel justified in harboring some contempt for women as weak-willed and indecisive.

*Fourth Joke.*

A man meets an aged friend wandering the streets, agitated and confused. Alarmed, he asks, "What's wrong?" The aged friend replies, "It's terrible. As you know, I have finally become a wealthy man, and I can have whatever my heart desires. So I bought this lovely penthouse with a four-way view, furnished it no expense spared, and I found this beautiful and sexy young woman who finds me so desirable. I married her and moved her into this apartment where, with open arms, she waits every day for the moment I return from the office." The friend then asks, "What could be wrong with that? Why does that upset you so?" With tears running down his cheeks, the old man answers, "I can't remember where I live."

The structure of this joke resembles that of the Lipschitz joke. On the surface, the butt of the joke is the rich old man. Unconsciously the memory lapse implies sexual impotence, perhaps even punitive castration for the implied narcissistically abusive, power-ridden, materialistic father-daughter incest that would, he seems to hope, sustain or restore the virility of his younger years and stave off death.

In unconscious fantasy, the forbidden sexual relation might also be masking a reversal of generations, in that the rich old man's marriage to a young woman could be a disguised version of the ordinary oedipal son's unconscious fantasy of omnipotent gratification of his incestuous wishes with an older woman. On a more primordial level, that reversal would pave the way for the old man's being fed and cared for by mother rather than feeding and caring for a child.

Additionally, a reversal of generations is often implied in relational conflicts over activity and passivity. We might say that the joke shows Father Time avenging himself on the perennially incestuous son.

The joke is on the man in yet another sense. It is implied that hubristic liaisons designed to be proof against age, disablement, and death must be punished by failure. Failing memory symbolizes the way from the cradle to the conjugal bed and on to the grave. Following Freud's (1926) proposition that death is fleshed out in unconscious fantasy in terms of the infantile danger situations, analysts would regard excessive concern with death as manifest or screen content that implies unconscious dread of castration and superego condemnation, the earlier danger situations of loss of love and loss of the love object (the young woman as mother figure), and the ultimate danger of annihilation. Additionally, analysis might have to take account of fantasies of omnipotence being shattered (being unable to reverse the clock) and the frustration of the greedy desire to "have it all!"

The specter of death might also enter enjoyment of the joke by the back door, for the situation is one in which the lusty young woman might be sucking the life out of the elderly man. In clinical work as well as folklore (for example, about male athletic performance), analysts encounter many versions of the anxiety-ridden fantasy that the female body is not only all-powerful but also depleting. This fantasy is based on infantile conceptions of the mother's sexual body as potentially dangerous. The fearful fantasies of the maternal body developed by boys and girls alike can only be partially or unstably mastered during development.

Two final notes about this joke: first, it must be said that, whatever the old man's plight, the development of this gender joke can also be taken to suggest the figure of the woman who sells herself—once again, the woman as whore. According to our social conventions and the man's advanced age, the marriage portrayed is not likely to be based on the woman's readiness for, or interest in, psychosexually mature love. She might not feel love at all. Conceivably, the narcissism of her self-seeking exceeds the old man's narcissism in "buying" her. Thus, this match could well be the kind that usually meets with general skepticism and dire predictions of material exploitation, cuckoldry, and failure. And so some listeners to the joke might well experience the young wife/whore as a powerful and exploitative figure, a wily young woman getting a free ride.

Secondly, the joke can be taken to signify one version of oedipal victory in its assault on parental sexuality. The child's wish to deny their exclusive and independent sexual union as well as repress its own oedipal wishes is realized in the figure of the husband who cannot remember, therefore cannot make it home, therefore cannot "make it" in bed. In the end, no conjugal couple remains to trouble the child.

## WOMAN AS AVENGER

The analysis of the first set of jokes, though focused on the figure of woman as whore, repeatedly and not unexpectedly brought in themes of women's power and men's exaggerated unconscious fear of that power's controlling and destructive potential. This second set of jokes presents these unconsciously frightening themes more openly and forcefully.

*Fifth Joke.*

A flasher accosts an elderly Jewish woman on the streets of Miami Beach. He throws open his raincoat and stands there fully exposed. She takes a look, shakes her head disapprovingly, and snaps at him, "You call that a lining!?"

Instead of registering sexual shock, embarrassment, or fright, the woman's response disempowers the flasher. Reducing him to a boy-like object of criticism—someone who can't look after himself—she nullifies his seeming attempt at phallic display and assault. By ignoring his "sexual" exhibition, she symbolically castrates him. An analyst, using familiar clinical interpretation as a basis, would promptly add that at that moment the flasher is also being confronted with the castratedness that, unconsciously, he is trying to negate by exposing his organ in a shocking manner. He is being told, "Sexually, you have nothing, and so you can mean nothing to a woman."

Viewing the joke broadly, the flasher's entire personhood is crushed. In one instant he becomes a nonperson, for in our conventional world of polarized gender roles, the woman's response implies the ultimate putdown: being turned into a derogated female who, *having* "nothing" where the man has a penis, *is* "nothing." We see here the woman taking revenge on the man on two fronts at once—or taking two revenges on one "front."

Upon further analysis, the joke also can be understood to imply denial of parental sexuality. It works this way: by portraying the woman as sexually unresponsive—no shock, no interest, no arousal, no threat of parental coupling—the symbolic mother is made sexless. Here, then, is the clinically familiar splitting of the maternal object: idealization of the virgin mother and derogation of the sexually faithless and degraded mother (see, in this regard, Freud 1912).

In sum, we may understand this joke to be playing on the unconscious fantasies and their associated anxieties of both sexes. Both the man and the woman are aggressors and victims and both get what is coming to them. Those listeners who suffer too much from conflict in any of these connections either will not find the joke funny at all or will feel ill at ease when they laugh.

Before leaving this devitalized scene, we must note a detail—again a Jewish woman—that raises once more the previously mentioned question of a joke's capacity to play on culturally loaded unconscious fantasies conducive to prejudice or self-mockery. The sixth joke does the same.

*Sixth Joke.*

A cleaned-up version of the flasher joke tells of a Jewish mother who gives her son two ties as a birthday present. Hoping to please her when he next visits her, he makes a point of wearing one of the ties, only to be challenged by her accusation in question form, "What's wrong? You don't like the other tie?!"

Again, the "boy's" (seductive? reparative?) approach to mother is repulsed, and he is left not only helplessly thwarted but having to deal with both her stimulation of his guilt feelings over his ingratitude and his sense that he can never satisfy her need for love or gratitude. Underlying these factors would be his sense, retained from boyhood, of inability to satisfy her sexually owing to the smallness of both his penis and his self relative to her emotional and sexual grandeur. Unconsciously, this clinically well-known concern persists into many men's adult years and adds impetus to their compensatory need to prove their phallic prowess or their self-protective retreat from the sphere of heterosexual activity.

Viewed more broadly, the joke also suggests that any expression of autonomy on the son's part (his taste in ties) is painful to the maternal figure. Again, there is suggested the primordial powerful, threatening, potentially depleting or engulfing mother. At the same time we seem once again to have before us the asexual mother, she who cannot be responsive to a loving or seductive approach. In the unconscious internal world, these contradictions raise no problem (Freud 1915b). In every respect, then, she will stimulate both struggles against dependency and pressured demonstrations of power.

As with the flasher joke, it is the pointed putdown of the son that indicates the operation of vengeance. In this instance, the mother's weapon is a common version of masochism: she wounds others through her readiness to feel hurt and aggrieved. However, it would be inexact and inadequate to think that the joke merely portrays women's masked sadism toward men or the sadism of mothers toward sons on whatever developmental level they may be being considered and however real or imagined her feelings and behavior may be. For to see it in these ways is to see it out of our cultural-historical context. Once situated in this context, we realize that we must take into account what has been emphasized throughout this chapter: how commonly women are the victims of men's anxiously narcissistic assertions of sexual and material power, and how often men use their power to extort women's emotions of every kind while they remain consciously self-absorbed, uncomprehending and, in a deep sense, unmoved. Consequently, it is necessary to view female sadomasochistic tactics and strategies as socially reinforced, relational phenomena. However rooted this dynamic may be in the unconscious infantile fantasies of men and women, it must also be seen as a response to men's socially endorsed provocations.

Furthermore, it would be arbitrary and simplistic to consider infantile fantasies and social reinforcement separate issues, for early and fantastic modes of constructing experience are not impervious to social-relational processes of childrearing, and later events in human relationships are known to have powerful unconscious effects of their own even if they do gain much of their force from infantile prototypes.

*Seventh Joke.*

In one of her routines, Mae West, after a quick glance at the crotch of a man who has just encountered her, asks him, "Is that a pistol in your pocket or are you just glad to see me?"

The posture Mae West assumes at this moment bears on many problematic aspects of heterosexual relations. In one respect, she presents us with the image of woman as seductress-witch: she who controls the man by seizing the initiative in looks and words and thereby arouses and controls his desire. Defying convention, the witch usurps the conventional male prerogative of forwardness in relation to women. Glorying in the role of pariah, Mae West shatters the mold of the passive-receptive and potentially victimized woman. With regard to pleasure and power, she denies herself nothing. For many men, being greeted in so forward a way is wildly exciting; it corresponds to the adolescent boy's fantasies of overwhelmingly forceful seduction by a powerful and experienced woman. When Mae West offers a mode of relationship that reverses conventional sexual roles, the man's exposed and passive desire is then analogous to the stereotypical modesty of the maiden in the process of being undone by the forceful man. In this respect, latent female identification gains some expression in this gender joke, as does a common masturbation fantasy of boys and men.

Where does female vengeance fit into this account of the joke's potentially comic effect? It does so by a woman's daring to usurp male power and initiative and reduce the male to another obedient stud, or a wishful boy. It further implies his castration and the powerful woman's acquisition of a phallic trophy. This woman will not accept the role of helpless victim of men that many aspects of society seem designed to impose on her. With reference to the pistol, we might say that, in more than one way, she *disarms* the man. By camouflaging her aggressive moves with seductiveness, she presents herself as both frightening and desirable, perhaps even exciting in her being threatening.

In another respect, Mae West figures as a campy yet powerful advocate of women's liberation. One might say that her way is the way of parody. It has been suggested by Judith Butler (1990) that, in this primarily phallocentric world, parody can be used to expose and ridicule the order of things; parody may even be one of the few effective means available to women to contribute constructively to change in sexual politics. In Mae West's parody, she does not repress her hostility; she merely masks it in sexually toned "laughing matters." Nor does she renounce her own libidinous interest in men; instead, it is part of her sexualizing strategy to take control and obtain gratification by focusing interest on the man's strategy to take control. One might say that she has found a way to mix sexual politics with pleasure.

Finally, in her own well-corseted (armored) way, she also becomes the all-powerful mother figure of early fantasy life. In this respect, she is also for some women an object of envy and rivalry, and on that account, either not entertaining at all or a source of uneasy amusement.

## DISCUSSION

It might seem to the skeptic that there are hardly any limits on psychoanalytic interpretations of stories—in the present case, jokes. Essays in the realm of applied psychoanalysis cannot claim to lead to the relatively firm and specific, though still provisional conclusions that are often reached in clinical work. Nor can they escape sounding formulaic. I believe that there is reason to be somewhat skeptical in this regard. However, I also believe, as I have argued elsewhere (1988), that the line between applied and clinical analysis is not as clear as many analysts believe it to be; for both approaches are firmly, even if not completely, guided and regulated by a specific psychoanalytic method and interpretive frames of reference.

The line between the clinical and the applied is blurred in another way, too. By showing how apparently straightforward narratives contain considerable unarticulated complexity of meaning and motive, as I have just done with regard to gender jokes, applied analysis is like clinical work in that it highlights latent contradictions, confusions, conflicts, and compromises in human existence.

Nevertheless, it is especially in clinical practice that one gets to be most cognizant of the forms, layering, intensities, and variability of the dynamic variables in play. Consequently, clinicians can articulate and adapt to individual differences and individualize each analysis creatively. This creative individualization cannot be accomplished to the same extent when one is considering only the specimens of applied analysis. Therefore, in this respect the applied analysis of jokes cannot go as far as clinical analysis. But, if it is developed with reasonable complexity, and if it remains tentative enough to show respect for the probable persuasiveness of alternative interpretations, applied analysis can establish in readers or clinicians a state of preparedness, a set of expectancies appropriate to their school of analytic thought. They will then be readier than before to understand the type and degree of responsiveness or aversion that jokes or other cultural productions stimulate. If not grandiose in their aspirations, applied analysts will not regard their own interpretations as conclusive evidence and so will refrain from formulating universalized propositions.

Beyond recognizing limits, the applied analyst must ask how the variables used in explanations are to be layered. For example, should power be regarded as superordinate, subordinate, or on the same level as sex and aggression? The same question may be asked about materialistic, class-oriented, and bigoted factors. In my view, hierarchic arrangements of these reference points are best regarded as epistemological and methodological narrative strategies played out in narrative forms. There is no one correct way, for there are no absolute foundations on which all must agree, for the designations right and wrong apply *within* one of the various systems of thought. Each stratification yields its own insights and blindness, its own profits and losses. Also, it is more than likely that the choice of any one strategy expresses commitments to certain social and personal values and the aims they generate, and thereby engagement in a certain kind of world-making. Consequently, although analysts may refer to sex, power, ethnic, class, *and* material factors as aspects of a joke in order to understand it in a complex way, they are also bracketing major questions of priority in the realm of method and interpretation.

## CONCLUDING REMARKS

First, I reemphasize the contributions of Ernst Kris (1952). Individual variations in the way jokes are received can be understood by analyzing how close each joke comes to incompletely mastered conflicts. The primary infantile conflicts that jokes touch on are best regarded as never fully mastered or resolved. Consequently, there is always room for, if not a basic need for, such forms of social play as joke telling. People can use jokes that provide the relief and reassurance of *remastering*—if not achieving full mastery, at least attaining some momentary sense of emotional security or confidence.

Bias is abundantly present in gender jokes as it is in every one of our social institutions and practices: literature, business, academia, and so on. I have tried to show its multiple manifestations in jokes, and at the same time to show the presence in these jokes of bias based on age, social status, material possession, and ethnicity. Interpreting these jokes in this complex manner indicates how full they are with signs of unconscious conflict. When successfully funny, these jokes touch on old conflicts that are neither completely mastered nor acutely threatening.

On this basis, well-analyzed analysts, like their well-analyzed patients, may and do still enjoy gender jokes. For no one can safely claim to have so far transcended the powerful fantasies and conflicts of childhood, the complications of exercises of power, and all those encounters with sexual and social-class bias and material and societal disadvantage, as to be entirely immune to the wit, the humor, the self-mockery, and the prejudices and grievances expressed and implied in gender jokes of any quality.

# PART III

An Overview

# Introduction to Part III

This concluding section of *Insight and Interpretation* was first presented (in somewhat less developed form) as one of a group of papers at a meeting of psychoanalysts and philosophers in the Philosophy Department of Columbia University, sponsored by that Department and the Columbia University Center for Psychoanalytic Training and Research. The meeting, including participants from outside Columbia University, was designed to promote dialogue between the two disciplines. In suiting my essay to that context, I tried to make my understanding of psychoanalysis as intelligible to philosophers as possible. I devoted the presentation to careful explication of the assumptions, language, and methods on the basis of which psychoanalysts arrive at their insights and interpretations. In this effort, I drew upon my many writings on the theory and practice of psychoanalysis, *the same ones that have been alluded to throughout this book.* Upon reviewing this talk today, it seems to sum up the foundational ideas of *Insight and Interpretation.* It also shows the reader where I have been and my present location in my continuing travels through the ever-evolving discipline of psychoanalysis.

# 9

# Knowing Another Person
# Psychoanalytically

This chapter concerns the nature of what we analysts know or believe we know, how we get to know it and justify our knowledge claims, and how to understand the differences among us in the claims we make. Although, at first glance, these topics might seem to those familiar with psychoanalysis so obvious and already well-discussed as to require no extended exposition here, when considered in depth they will be found to be at the center of intellectually demanding and unending controversy, perhaps even confronting us finally with basic issues in our discipline that cannot be resolved. Far from being merely an unnecessary review of well-known aspects of psychoanalytic work, my discussion will include complex and debatable considerations of epistemology, methodology, and system building.

I enter this troubled domain believing that analysts have not yet thought through sufficiently the difficult issues that underlie many familiar and often taken for granted assumptions about psychoanalytic knowledge. I am also aware that these considerations will never reach a final stage owing to the constantly changing contexts of critical thought in which the key concepts of psychoanalysis must be reconsidered and reformulated if our discipline is to remain relevant to a rapidly changing standards of sound, though still controversial, critical thought.

## WHAT WE CLAIM TO KNOW

Ordinarily, when you claim to know someone, you are asserting only that you have developed a version of him or her that is stable enough to be identifiable and communicable in some way; for you cannot claim that your version is the only version possible or desirable in every context. At least you cannot make that claim legitimately, though many do, of course, as when they assert that they know someone like an open book—as though a book allows only one way to read it—or when, as some analysts do, you deliver polished, single-minded, all-inclusive, and doubt-free case formulations.

It is important to remember that it is always possible, and it may become desirable in another context of persons, circumstances, aims, and interests, to construct a different version of someone you say you know. In that case, you will then know him or her in another way, say, as a friend and not merely as a distant relative. Furthermore, others usually construct their own, more or less different versions of that person and pit them against yours. The infinitive "to know" is itself so ambiguous—it covers everything from casual social acquaintance to biblical sexual intimacy—that its use virtually serves warning to take nothing for granted about what is being claimed.

Although the idea of a person, too, may be considered similarly problematic in that its defining characteristics, such as its boundaries, may be specified variously by different observers or by the object of observation himself or herself, I will use it here in its indexical sense. That is to say, I will use it as a pointer, a word that means no more than "I," "you," "he," and "she"—pronouns that in themselves claim nothing whatsoever about contents, boundaries, and implications of identities.

The psychoanalyst's professional career is devoted to constructing highly specialized versions of other persons undergoing analysis, that is, to know each analysand *psychoanalytically*. That form of knowing is designed and regulated by a more or less systematized set of principles of interpretation. These principles are formulated in the analyst's own lexicon (not that they are ordinarily communicated to analysands that way), and they are implemented through an adequately specified assortment of desirable methods that develop such psychoanalytically significant themes as sex, aggression, anxiety, guilt, shame, depression, symptoms, and inhibitions. These themes are conceived broadly enough to allow considerable individualized detailing of the analysand's problem-ridden experiences.

For many years, I understood *psychoanalysis* to mean ego-psychological Freudian analysis, and in many ways I have retained that understanding. However, in recent years I have been accommodating this psychoanalysis to the requirements of the version of Kleinian analysis that has evolved in London in recent decades. Yet other versions of psychoanalysis—for example, self psychological, relational, existential—have been developed during the past century. Each has found its adherents, and each version has had some influence on the others. Consequently, there now exist alternative, more or less distinct and systematized ways of knowing another person psychoanalytically. It should therefore be understood that, in this chapter, I am describing *my* favored version of psychoanalysis. Although, to retain some focus, I will not now review and discuss alternative conceptions, I will take further note of them later in this chapter. My version is not unique.

Before concluding this chapter, I will move closer to practice so that my relatively abstract and generalized discussion will be grounded in the consulting room. Specifically, I will review the main features of the *interpretation of defense*, that crucial aspect of clinical psychoanalysis. Leading up to that section will be discussions of my general orientation to interpretation, the interpretation of actions in their contexts, interpretation as narrative, the important role of systematized theory in shaping interpretive narratives, and intersubjective aspects of psychoanalytic knowing—a recurring, subordinate theme in this book.

## INTERPRETATION

My understanding of interpretation has been developed through reflecting on my clinical experience, studying the psychoanalytic literature, and reading in other disciplines in which interpretation has been a continuing preoccupation and area of controversy: historiography, literary theory, anthropology, feminist writings, general psychology, and philosophy in its own right and as it has been brought to bear on controversies within these other disciplines. There is no universal agreement to be found within any of these disciplines, nor within the interdisciplinary efforts that have been made, for example, by feminist thinkers. Consequently, I have had to make selective use of all that I have encountered—as I have understood it—and I acknowledge at once my recognition that each of the formulations to be proposed here is contestable.

My selection has been guided by the general aim of developing an alternative to what I regard as Freud's mostly mechanistic and empiricist *conceptualization* of psychoanalysis. I believe that Freud's dominant conception does not do justice to the methods and insights that have evolved from his works of creative genius. For the most part, contemporary discourse in the other disciplines I just mentioned has moved beyond the later nineteenth century discourse favored by Freud. That earlier discourse featured the models, concepts, metaphors, evidential criteria, and modes of explanation appropriate to laboratories, industrial machines, and early Darwinism. At any rate, as I have argued at length elsewhere (1976, 1978, 1983, 1992, 1994, 1995, 1997a), these, along with metaphors drawn from mythology, were Freud's leading sources for his theoretical formulations.

I consider interpretation to be the essential operation involved in getting to know. What we know is not the fact of the matter plain and simple; rather, it is our *interpretation* of whatever is the case. For there is no direct access to whatever is the case. We deal only with constructed versions of it.

I also believe, contrary to Freud's theorizing, that it is fruitful to think of the clinical analyst as working with another *person*—not with a mind and not with a mental apparatus. Analysts work *within* a specialized form of human relationship and simultaneously they work *on* that relationship. They aim to define *in the analytic way* their analysands' characteristic unconscious modes of thought and feeling and to help them recognize where and how these modes contribute significantly to the problems for which they have sought help. When successful—for the evidence needed for sound interpretation is hard won and often not entirely conclusive and usually obtained in the face of analysands' strong defenses against insight and change—despair and destructiveness give way to adaptive efforts. Then, the painfulness of undertaking basic change become tolerable enough to allow movement into more creative realms of action, however anxiously and erratically this may be done.

Analysts have developed more or less systematic approaches to their work. Each approach features formats and modes of conduct designed to help them develop the kind of psychoanalytic knowledge they believe appropriate. They get to know their analysands and especially their problems in ways that differ significantly, though not totally, from knowledge of persons acquired in other social and occupational contexts, say, as family members, friends, employees, or neighbors. Although one or another version of common sense is always a significant part of this growing knowledge, it is not so much its defining feature as it sometimes seems to be.

Some features of constructing psychoanalytic knowledge have been brought out earlier. In Chapter 1, I referred to insight into insight, by which I pointed to the analyst's unflagging interest both in what it means to the analysand to understand and to be understood and her or his interest in what it means personally to be engaged in creating meaning or new meaning about another person and for that person. For, as mentioned, the analytic enterprise lends itself to being unconsciously experienced by the analyst, as by the analysand, as invasive, plundering, voyeuristic, nurturant, seductive, punitive, and so on. The often arduous and disciplined pursuit of insight into insight is a crucial aspect of a beneficial analysis (see in this regard Joseph 1983).

The analyst's self-knowledge, too, may increase during the clinical process. Again, it will be knowledge conceptualized along psychoanalytic lines. That knowledge is acquired by the analyst's reflecting on his or her own manner of relating to a specific analysand in specific contexts. Reflection is called for especially if this way of relating has been introducing restrictions of activity or understanding, undue emphases, or overreactions; for the thoughtful analyst realizes that these disruptive features must be understood and regulated for two main reasons: to protect the analysis from becoming mainly a narcissistic vehicle for the analyst's own self-expression and to enhance the analysis by teasing out the analysand's influence on one's own feeling states and actions as analyst.

Ideally, the analyst constructs contexts and chooses designations that avoid expressing what, for purely personal reasons, he or she thinks or feels about what seems to be going on. Instead, the analyst aims at formulating the analytically most efficacious statement of the analysand's currently prevailing intentions, fantasies, conflicts, or emotional experiences.

As I just indicated, other important gains result from analysts' reflections on their manner of relating to specific analysands. In many instances, their self-analyses of the personal repercussions of their work increase their understanding of the part played by their analysands in stimulating their emotional and intellectual responses. By now, analysts have discussed often and at length the analysand's influence on the analyst, an influence that is achieved in numerous subtle and not so subtle ways (see, for example, the recent discussion by Kantrowitz 2002). This aspect of the work has been taken up in several previous chapters, especially Chapter 5.

Analyzing within this general orientation is the basis for my entitling this chapter not "Knowing Other Minds" but "Knowing Another Person *Psychoanalytically*." But, as I have already asserted, it is in keeping with both contemporary critical thought and acknowledgment of the variety of psychoanalytic systems that have been developed, never to claim that there is only one true way of knowing anything or anyone psychoanalytically. No one owns the word "psychoanalysis." Even within each school of thought, one encounters heterogeneity of understanding and interpretation, though typically less of it there than among the various schools. Therefore, I emphasize again that I am presenting *my* version. Mine is not the only possible or legitimate version, and because none of the existing systems is entirely distinct from the others, my version will be found to resemble others in many respects.

This acknowledged, I believe I am free to state the details of this version in straightforward, often confident terms. The simple affirmations that follow should not be taken as lapses into the realist position usually taken by Freud in his official pronouncements, though not always in his margins. My orientation remains hermeneutic and therefore always provisional and open to what I (1985) have called comparative analysis.

## INTERPRETING ACTIONS IN THEIR CONTEXTS

Analysands engage in a variety of actions during their analytic sessions. They talk or fall silent. They remember and forget selectively. They emote freely and reflect thoughtfully. They develop fantasies or stick to circumstantial accounts of daily events. They reveal what they think and feel about the analyst or they avoid that subject like the plague. There is no end to the variations in what they do. It is warranted to refer to all of these instances as actions (Schafer 1976, 1983). They are performative, that is, things analysands do, not things that happen to them. The analyst assumes that whatever is done is done on the basis of the potentially interpretable beliefs and desires that constitute intentionality.

Happenings—things not intended by the subject—are, of course, often part of the story, for example, floods, storms, traffic jams, drunken drivers, and physiological signs of wasting, depression, and embarrassment. Analytically, however, the story does not end there, for actions retain a place in these stories, too, at least in the meanings the analysand invests in these happenings—punishment, confession, betrayal by Fate—and perhaps in the analysands having exposed themselves unduly or their having exploited "the accidental." Often, no clear line can be drawn between happenings-as-experienced and other actions.

This orientation to action requires the analyst to bear in mind that however self-evident the name of each action might seem to be, that action does not name or describe itself. First, its name is implied in what analysands seem to be telling and enacting during their sessions. Subsequently, and for analytic purposes, the analyst might and often does rename or retell it in another way. The analyst's choice of name or description *selectively* retells the things analysands do in speech, thought, expressive movement, or other physical activity. The analyst's choices, if they are not already interpretations, are usually intended to help prepare the ground for interpretation.

For instance, what the analysand names a lapse of attention, the analyst might rename a sign of aversion to what the analyst is saying. Even the simple designations of actions I mentioned a moment ago—talk, remember, reflect, and so forth—were chosen names, not natural or inevitable names. To take another example: in one context, the analyst might say that an analysand who is moving quickly from one topic to another seemingly at random is showing the analyst a feeling of being confused and, in another context, the analyst might say that these shifts of topic are defensive, the analysand using them to prevent the development of strong and threatening emotions. Naming expresses understanding and intention, and it is often used for defensive purposes.

Thus, the analysand's naming or description that initially renders an action available for thought and speech should itself be considered an interpretation, though it might not be cast in developed psychoanalytic form. For instance, in the example I just gave—rapid changing of topics—the analysand might have said, "I'm just rambling" prior to the analyst's pointing out the defensive use of the rapid changes: both designations—rambling and defending—are interpretations, each true in its way, though as a rule only the analyst's has the potential to further the analytic work. For "rambling" is likely to be an interpretation that both disclaims responsibility for this turn of events and defies the analyst to make sense of it.

Each description of an action issues from a *context* of understanding, and it implies that context. We are constantly being reminded that, to be fair or objective, we should not consider things out of context. However, no one of these things comes packaged in a natural context. Contexts of understanding do not present themselves ready-made; they must be constructed, and all that is usable for these constructions are previous interpretations *made in their contexts*. That is to say, to construct contexts, analysts must draw on many aspects of their constructed understanding of the preceding analytic dialogue. Often, they do this aspect of the work preconsciously, drawing on the familiarity that comes with training, experience, and the continuing work with the analysand. Preconscious preparation often makes it seem that they do it without thinking about it—as though purely intuitively. This is illusion.

Working within a constructed context, the analyst does not take for granted what convention might suggest is one and the same action, say, the analysand's doing some self-analysis on the couch. In doing so, the analysand might, in one context, be thought to be defensively warding off the analyst's interventions; in another context, thought to be making a competitive show of understanding; in a third, warding off any show of dependency; in a fourth, evidencing a new spirit of collaboration; and in a fifth, "all of the above" to one or another degree and in a hierarchized manner that throws light on core problems.

The point is that establishing a context is itself part of the interpretive process. When, for example, the analyst specifies that it is competitiveness that is being enacted by the analysand's doing some self-analysis, he or she is selecting and developing that version of it that seems best suited to enhance analytic understanding *at that time*. Ideally, the analyst also remains alert for signs that a new context is developing or at least that the one in use requires revision or supplementation and that new descriptions for actions might now be required. The analyst's maintaining too narrow or fixed a focus can become a huge obstacle to further analysis. It is usually difficult to foretell the exact route by which access will be gained to further significant analytic material.

## NARRATION

Elsewhere (1983, 1992), I have developed the case for the narrativity of this contextual telling and retelling of analysands' actions and experiences of happenings. This narrative construction of descriptions and interpretations helps develop a systematically coherent and consistent account while leaving room for revision, supplementation, and novelty.

My argument on behalf of narration centers on the following considerations. Because actions exist only under a description, the analyst necessarily chooses each of his or her retellings from an array of possible descriptions. As mentioned, the analyst's choice of description is usually based on contexts he or she has constructed out of previously constructed versions of actions. So far as possible and sensible, the analyst fits the local choices into already developed larger accounts, in that way contributing toward a comprehensive, consistent, coherent, but still provisional version of the analysand's functioning in the current clinical situation as well as in comparable situations in extra-analytic life. In developing this version, the analyst focuses especially on conflictual, disturbed, and painful experiences that limit integrative, adaptive, and creative thinking and action in the surrounding world. Especially important are narrativized interpretations of what seems to be being experienced unconsciously and perhaps enacted in the analytic relationship. However it might be achieved, each version is only one of a number of ways of telling it.

The analyst is not narrating in the conventional sense of telling make-believe stories designed to help the analysand feel better; for the analyst aims to formulate what he or she believes seems to be true within the kind of psychoanalytic perspective being employed. Nor is the analyst necessarily narrating in the conventional sense of telling a story with a beginning, middle, and end, for one may speak of narration when developing a specific verbal version of one or more events or observations and perhaps integrating this version with others that have already been formulated, however provisionally. The items used are given significance within a psychoanalytically conceived narrative context of difficulties being presented by the analysand.

Many analysts seem to have had trouble accepting this understanding of the term narration. I believe that some of this difficulty is attributable to the mistaken inference that narration is somehow an alternative to trying to make true statements. Some of the difficulty, however, may be attributable to the fact that ordinary language favors ocular metaphors to convey the development of understanding and formulation (see Chapter 3). I refer to our thinking and speaking in ordinary language of taking a point of view, having a perspective, reflecting, and seeing things one way rather than another; similarly, we refer to insight and putting things in a new light, and we say, "I see what you mean," and so on.

Ocular metaphors take precedence in psychoanalytic discourse, too, even though it is obvious that the analytic process is one that deals in optional verbal constructions of what is taken to be true or the truth-value of which is worth considering further. I believe that *narrating* is harder to accept than *seeing* partly because it renders thought in a form that seems less concrete and therefore less obvious or "given" than the visual-spatial, which is a form that seems to be directly connected to the sense organs. That is to say, the sense organ metaphor is favored because, prereflectively, it seems to guarantee unmediated contact with a "true" world as contrasted with a "possible" world.

The sensory metaphor implies two interlocking and seemingly unquestionable beliefs: that the sensory embodiment of understanding presents nature directly, that is, unmediated by thought, and that "nature" is itself a given, immediately accessible, uncon-structed, unchanging world. Additionally, by claiming only to see what is there, the analyst assumes less responsibility than he or she does when communicating a new, psychoanalytic version of the analysand's communications.

For reasons already given, neither of these beliefs holds water. Therefore, I consider the idea of narration better suited than vision to discuss psychoanalytic work. We do, after all, have reason to refer to psychoanalysis as "the talking cure."

## CONTEXTS AND THEORIES

I mentioned that the analyst derives an interpretive descrip-tion of the analysand's actions within a context of understanding that is itself the product of interpretations. To amplify this contex-tual emphasis, it should be emphasized that everything depends on the kind of context of understanding that the analyst favors in his or her way of doing analysis. Each context is favored in response to a number of major influences. These influences include much more than the conventionally understood or commonsense implications of the explicit material covered by the preceding analytic dialogue. They include what the analyst has already come to accept or accept provisionally as analytically derived knowledge of the analysand's past and present life, including life within the analysis itself.

This knowledge of the analysand is far from being theory-free. To the extent that the analyst thinks systematically, theory will have been playing a major regulative role in what he or she has selected from the material being relayed by the analysand verbally and nonverbally and from how he or she formulated it and orga-nized it. The analytic narrative has been and will be both limited and enhanced by it theoretical guidelines.

Many or most analysts do claim allegiance to a school of sys-tematic analytic thought, and each school qualifies as a school by being different to some significant extent from others in its presup-positions about motivations, human development, psychopathol-

ogy, and the analytic process. Also, each school has been sufficiently thought through, conceptualized, and linked to technical issues to qualify as a distinctive form of conducting psychoanalysis. In
narrative terms, one can say that each school has its overarching
metanarratives and its set of preferred storylines for developing contexts and deriving interpretations within these contexts.

More than that, each systematic approach has its rules of evidence, some explicit, some tacitly understood, and all of them consistent with the identifying features of the school of thought that
they represent. On this basis, one can always apply criteria of quality
to individual instances of analytic work. Within each school, analysts can usually differentiate what is clearly valid, coherent, or consistent and what is grossly invalid, incoherent, or inconsistent. They
can agree on an analyst's having missed the point or having blurred
it or got it just right. There is, of course, always room in the middle
for disagreement over interpretation. This is so because the psychoanalytic rules of evidence are never that exacting or exclusive.

Also to be noted is this: the rules of any one school are not
unique even though each is, as I mentioned, different enough from
the rules of others for one to recognize their belonging together.
The different schools are not so sharply or completely set off from
one another that they are totally self-validating and impervious to
any critique at all. To a large extent, each school has by now taken
over concepts and rules of evidence from the others, from
commonsense understanding of people and relationships, and from
general logic. Not every principle or connection has been derived
within the system; nor need it be stated in a strictly technical form.

Consequently, it is not unusual that instances of clinical work,
when presented to a group of analysts of differing theoretical persuasions, lead the participants into relatively harmonious discussions.
Then, analysts of one school might say of the work of another
school, "I don't see what is so different about that!", "But we already
knew that!", or "Are we really that different?!" It is, however, best
not to lose sight of the differences among the varied schools of psychoanalytic thought. Despite the many superficial family resemblances and overlaps one may note, larger contexts of thought and

interpretation stand in the way of claiming true family membership. This area of unclear boundaries and superficial family resemblances has not yet been adequately explored.

I emphasize this point of difference within apparent harmony here mainly to make it clear that it is only systematization that raises clinical presentation and discussion to the level on which useful critiques can be developed. On that level, one does not simply have to take or reject the other's word for whatever is being conveyed, and one is no longer restricted to impressions of the moment. Only if these conditions are met can psychoanalysis claim to be a discipline. Far-ranging eclecticism or too ready blurring of differences seriously compromises the idea of psychoanalysis as a discipline that yields communicable knowledge of other persons. My remarks have been oriented toward system-regulated analytic work. In this regard, what has been called common ground is illusory.

## INTERSUBJECTIVITY

Currently, many analysts have begun putting special emphasis on personal influences on interpretation. These influences stem from the analyst's present personality makeup, including his or her reasons for being an analyst, quality of training, style of working, emotional sensitivity, intellectual facility, persistent positive and negative attitudes toward former supervisors and personal analysts, and especially current conceptions of and attitudes toward the specific analysand. It is no longer acceptable to marginalize or minimize these influences or treat them as aberrations. No longer can analysts present themselves as almost purely objective and always equally qualified observers of analysands' minds as revealed in free association and behavior. Often, however, analysts continue implicitly to present themselves in this aseptic way by making no mention of alternative interpretations, ambiguities, doubts, errors, and personal feelings and attitudes.

In my thinking, however, the greater problem today is not this purist image but rather the move toward the opposite extreme.

More and more analysts consider these personal influences so weighty that they insist that the interpretive process be regarded as altogether intersubjective. *Intersubjective* has no single definition, but it seems that the word is usually used to imply that, in the analytic situation, there can be no ultimate authority on what is real, objective, or distorted. Instead, sound procedure requires that a consensus be negotiated by the two personally engaged participants, neither one of them an objective participant. Each participant can only express a personal point of view (see, e.g., Gill 1994) or what I would call a personalized narrative preference.

I believe that this one conception of intersubjectivity exaggerates what ordinarily takes place in the analytic situation. It substitutes one part of it—the personal—for the whole and then arbitrarily forces an all-or-nothing theoretical choice. This rhetorical tactic short-circuits complex consideration of the conditions under which the analyst may legitimately claim the kind of objectivity that a systematic psychoanalytic approach makes possible, that is, the objectivity I have been trying to clarify in this essay and elsewhere. Chapter 5, on the subject of neutrality, deals with these and other aspects of the issues just mentioned.

## KNOWING AS CONSTRUCTING NARRATIVES: A SUMMARY

An interim summary of the points developed thus far should help the reader follow the reasoning in the promised section on the interpretation of defense, to which I will turn next. Psychoanalytic knowing is to be regarded as a specialized narrative developed in accord with the metanarratives and particularized storylines that define and implement a specific version of systematic psychoanalysis. The narrative action of knowing is accomplished by employing constructed and more or less system-regulated, coherent, and consistent contexts of understanding. The analyst establishes contexts and interventions in a certain way, uses organizing concepts and themes with certain interrelationships, and then links formulations in specific ways that establish hierarchies of importance. In this way the analyst is equipped to arrive at general accounts of the analysand with significant, though system-bound, truth-value.

Freud's metanarratives and storylines and their applications in specific acts of knowing are not those of the self psychologists; nor are they those of the object relations theorists. Although there is some overlap among the three, they remain distinguishable. In Freud's contributions, one deals with instinctual drives, the pleasure-unpleasure principle, the need of the developing organism to adapt to external reality by accepting its limitations and the pain it can inflict through frustration, deprivation, and physical distress or injury; also the increasing, frustration-induced use of one's inborn mental apparatus to test this reality and differentiate it from wishful fantasy and to employ repression and other defenses as well as prohibitions and self-punishments to consolidate a viable and effective mode of existence within the social reality of the given family and surround. The other two schools I mentioned—and they are not the only ones—formulate things more or less differently.

Whatever the approach, knowing is to be regarded as a construction. This construction instantiates the making of a specialized reality. That is to say, it yields a technical version of the analysand's reality and of the analysand's conventionalized and distinctive modes of constructing and maintaining that reality.

Critics of psychoanalysis belittle this technical formulation of the analysand's reality as jargon. Out of prejudice or naivete, they act as though commonsense language is the only or best language for intradisciplinary formulating and communicating knowledge of other persons. Commonsense language does, of course, have its major place in clinical and colloquial dialogue, and, as I've mentioned, it has its place in psychoanalytic theory, too; however, that point about language in practice and theory is too narrow to deal with the subtleties required to maintain an analytic discipline.

In narrative terms, knowing is telling an analysand's reality one way rather than another and being ready to specify and justify the evidence that has been used to tell it that way. Justification includes being ready to acknowledge that the evidence itself has been constructed to facilitate the analyst's relatively coherent and consistent development of his or her case-specific, favored psychoanalytic narrative. The analyst must also acknowledge the appearance of reductiveness and circularity in this process, but she or he is also ready to argue that much or all of this appearance is a manifestation of systematic thinking rather than formula-bound impersonality. Ideally, the analyst is also ready to formulate alternative accounts within his or her system of thought and to give reasons why, in a given context, it is advantageous to set aside these alternatives.

## INTERPRETING DEFENSE

To illustrate concretely what I have just been summarizing, I will now turn briefly to my account of a common way in which analysts interpret defense. In line with what has already been set forth, defense will be treated not as an entity found in nature but as a construction that is developed along the lines first laid down systematically by Freud in 1926 and then somewhat revised and supplemented by later psychoanalytic thinkers (A. Freud 1936, Fenichel 1941, Schafer 1968b). Bear in mind that the Freudian way is only one way to construe this aspect of the clinical process.

For example, an analysand might be considered by the analyst to be relying excessively on *idealization* in the transference to the analyst, for there seem to be too many and too lavish positive responses to the analyst and the analytic work. In the context of what has been understood up to this point in the analysis of this one person, the analyst might interpret this idealization in various ways, of which the following few are representative: the analysand might be trying to play on the analyst's vanity in order to gain acceptance and preferential treatment, in this way warding off feelings of unworthiness; the analysand might be entertaining semiprivate fantasies of being treated by a superanalyst, in that way validating self-aggrandizing tendencies and contradicting feelings of helplessness and insignificance; perhaps the idealization is being used to forestall conscious feelings of envy of the analyst or contempt, either of which, it is feared, might alienate the analyst on whom one also depends; perhaps idealization is being used sadistically to mock the analyst while appearing all innocence.

On his or her part, the analyst might be unconsciously courting this idealization for his or her own defensive purposes. The analyst might therefore remain oblivious to this use of idealization or just take it for granted as good reality testing, in that way avoiding recognition of personal insecurity and fallibility in working with that analysand or perhaps all analysands.

At different points in the analysis, depending on emotional cues given by both participants, on other evidence that has been developed along analytic lines, and further self-analysis by the analyst, the analyst might put the emphasis first on one of these constructions and later on another one. Ordinarily, the analyst will change emphasis during the analytic process, though not necessarily with the sense of making a correction; for sometimes it is a matter of the analyst's having defined further uses the analysand is now making of the idealization, or perhaps the analyst can now formulate more fully how the analysand has been making use of it all along and how he or she (the analyst) has been colluding unwittingly with the analysand's defensive strategy.

In each instance, idealizing qualifies as defensive in that it can be shown through contextual analysis that it is aimed at blocking out painful and disruptive experiences that stem from negative beliefs and feelings about the self and the analyst as experienced. These beliefs include personally unacceptable or intolerable actions one has engaged in or might engage in under less controlled conditions. In many instances, it will be implied that these beliefs are based on unconscious fantasies that are inadequately differentiated from conventionally realistic perceptions. Alternatively, these beliefs may be based on repressed deeds or events or persons in one's past as remembered or retold in the present—memory itself being very much a constructive process according to current psychological views of it.

Freud preferred the formulation of defense mechanisms against impulses or drive-derivatives, and he listed a series of them, including repression, undoing, projection, and regression. That way of putting it fit in with his drive theory and his wish to develop his metanarrative of psychoanalysis as a biologically based conflict theory. And it also fit in with Freud's other main preference, that for metanarratives that emphasized mechanism and its functional parts. However, the texts of his clinical examples show that the referents of his systematizing formulations were beliefs, intentions, feelings, wishes, memories, prohibitions, and the person's sense of helplessness in integrating them.

Additionally, practicing analysts have customarily referred to all kinds of actions and modes of function as defensive; they have not limited themselves to Freud's taxonomy of "defense mechanisms." For example, when analysts are working more freely, as Freud himself did in his clinical practice, they also refer to defensive bravado, defensive passivity, defensive heterosexual activity, and so on. The taxonomy has been retained over the years because Freud's formulations have proved their usefulness; however, some analysts have gone on to emphasize other mechanisms and some have introduced significantly different formulations (see, for example, Kohut 1984).

In the clinical situation, major defensive actions will come into play in the way the analysand tries to structure the analytic relationship. The analyst's own defensive tendencies may play some part in this development, although he or she is unlikely to be burdened by the intense sense of crisis, dread, and helplessness that afflicts the analysand. Consequently, the analyst is usually less defended and able to be better attuned than the analysand to the clinical situation and the opportunities it offers for understanding and for alternative and adaptive courses of action. In other words, working within his or her context of understanding—a context usually greatly clarified by personal analysis and supervision—the analyst is in a better position to analyze issues neutrally, that is, to give all sides of conflict a reasonably impartial and full hearing.

## CONCLUDING REMARKS

In the end, a great deal about the analysand remains unknown to the analyst. The gaps in knowledge may be attributed to the analytic dialogue's selective narrative development and its system-regulated nature. According to its slant on existence, systematic thinking both facilitates understanding and limits it. Systematic thinking is the torch that lights one's way into the darkness of the unconscious internal world, but it cannot illuminate everything. Not everything will have been of equal interest to the analyst, not everything will have been analytically accessible, and not everything will have been sufficiently conflictual to produce leads into unconscious fantasy and conflict. There will always be that which awaits further conceptual development before anyone can develop insight into it.

Also, there comes a time when terminating the analysis will seem to be preferable to continuing analytic exploration and working through of problems. Termination will be preferable for all kinds of reasons such as the analysand's changing life circumstances; a readiness on the analysand's part to begin living independently and, when necessary, making analytic sense independently; or mutual recognition that this analytic relationship has clearly reached a point of drastically diminishing returns. At that time, many areas of life, past and present, will have been covered, but not all. Many symptomatic developments will have been analyzed, but not all. Many significant relationships will have been reviewed, but not all. Because it is a specialized form of knowing, "knowing another person psychoanalytically" refers to a limited form of knowing. In this respect, of course, it is like other modes of knowing. In other respects, it is knowing that is unusally profound.

# References

Abelove, H., Bavale, M. R., and Halperin, D. M., eds. (1993). *The Lesbian and Gay Studies Reader*. New York and London: Routledge.

Abrams, S. (1996). Offerings and acceptances: technique and therapeutic action. *Psychoanalytic Study of the Child* 51:71–86.

Anderson, R. (1996). Putting the boot in: violent defences against depressive anxiety. In *The Contemporary Kleinians of London*, ed. R. Schafer, pp. 123–238. New York: International Universities Press.

Benjamin, W. (1969). *Illuminations: Essays and Reflections*, ed. H. Arendt. New York: Shocken Books.

Bion, W. (1959). Attacks on linking. *International Journal of Psycho-Analysis* 40:308–315.

Brenman Pick, I. (1985). Working through in the countertransference. *International Journal of Psycho-Analysis* 66:157–166. In *The Contemporary Kleinians of London*, ed. R. Schafer, pp. 348–369. New York: International Universities Press.

Britton, R. (1985). The missing link: parental sexuality in the Oedipus complex. In *The Oedipal Complex Today: Clinical Implications*, ed. J. Steiner, pp. 83–101. London: Karnac, 1989.

Butler, J. (1990). *Gender Trouble: Feminism and the Subversion of Identity.* New York and London: Routledge.

Dominici, T., and Lesser, R., eds. (1995). *Disorienting Sexuality: Psychoanalytic Reappraisal of Sexual Identities*, pp. 187–282. New York and London: Routledge.

Feldman, M. (1994). The Oedipus complex: manifestations in the inner world and the therapeutic situation. In *The Oedipus Complex Today: Clinical Implications*, ed. J. Steiner, pp. 103–128. London: Karnac.

Fenichel, O. (1941). *Problems of Psychoanalytic Technique.* New York: Psychoanalytic Quarterly.

Fliess, R. (1942). The metapsychology of the analyst. *Psychoanalytic Quarterly* 11:211–227.

Freud, A. (1936). *The Mechanisms of Defence.* New York: International Universities Press, 1946.

Freud, S. (1905a). Jokes and their relation to the unconscious. *Standard Edition* 8. London: Hogarth Press, 1960.

——— (1905b). Three essays on the theory of sexuality. *Standard Edition* 7:125–244.

——— (1907). The sexual enlightenment of children. *Standard Edition* 9:131–140.

——— (1908). On the sexual theories of children. *Standard Edition* 9:209–236.

——— (1912). On the universal tendency to debasement in the sphere of love. (Contributions to the psychology of love II.) *Standard Edition* 11:177–191. London: Hogarth Press, 1957.

——— (1914). Observations on transference love. (Further recommendations on the technique of psycho-analysis, III.) *Standard Edition* 12:157–171. London: Hogarth Press, 1958.

——— (1915a). Instincts and their vicissitudes. *Standard Edition* 14:109–140. London: Hogarth Press, 1957.

——— (1915b). The unconscious. *Standard Edition* 14:159–217.

——— (1915c). On narcissism: an introduction. *Standard Edition* 14:73–102. London: Hogarth Press, 1957.

——— (1917). Remembering, repeating, and working through. (Further recommendations on the technique of psycho-analysis.) *Standard Edition* 12:145–156.

——— (1921). Group psychology and the analysis of the ego. *Standard Edition* 18:69–143. London: Hogarth Press, 1957.

———— (1922). Some neurotic mechanisms in jealousy, paranoia and homosexuality. *Standard Edition* 18:223–232.

———— (1923). The ego and the id. *Standard Edition* 19:3–66. London: Hogarth Press, 1961.

———— (1926). Inhibition, symptoms, and anxiety. *Standard Edition* 20:77–175. London: Hogarth Press, 1959.

———— (1937). Analysis terminable and interminable. *Standard Edition* 23:216–254. London: Hogarth Press, 1964.

———— (1939). An outline of psychoanalysis. *Standard Edition* 23:144–207. London: Hogarth Press, 1964.

———— (1954). *The Origins of Psychoanalysis: Letters to Wilhelm Fliess*, trans. E. Mosbacher and J. Strachey. New York: Basic Books.

Friedman, R. J., and Natterson, J. M. (1999). Enactments: An intersubjectivist perspective. *Psychoanalytic Quarterly* 68:220–247.

Geertz, C. (1973). *The Interpretation of Cultures: Selected Essays*. New York: Basic Books.

Gill, M. M. (1994). *Psychoanalysis in Transition*. Hillsdale, NJ: Analytic Press.

Glover, E. (1931). The therapeutic effect of inexact interpretation: a contribution to the theory of suggestion. In *The Technique of Psychoanalysis*, ed. E. Glover, pp. 353–366. New York: International Universities Press, 1955.

Hartmann, H. (1939). *Ego Psychology and the Problem of Adaptation*, trans. D. Rapaport. New York: International Universities Press, 1958.

———— (1951). Technical implications of ego psychology. *Psychoanalytic Quarterly* 20:31–43.

———— (1960). *Psychoanalysis and Moral Values*. New York: International Universities Press.

———— (1964). *Essays on Ego Psychology: Selected Problems in Psychoanalytic Theory*. New York: International Universities Press.

Hartmann, H., Kris, E., and Loewenstein, R. M. (1964). Papers on psychoanalytic psychology (*Psychological Issues Monograph* No. 14). New York: International Universities Press.

Hartmann, H., and Loewenstein, R. M. (1962). Notes on the superego. *Psychoanalytic Study of the Child* 12:42–81.

Jacobson, E. (1964). *The Self and the Object World*. New York: International Universities Press.

Joseph, B. (1983). On understanding and not understanding. *International Journal of Psycho-Analysis* 64:291–298.

Kantrowitz, J. (2002). The external observer and the lens of the patient-analyst match. *International Journal of Psycho-Analysis* 83:339–350.

Klein, M. (1940). Mourning and its relation to manic-depressive states. In *Love, Guilt and Reparation and Other Works, 1921–1945*, pp. 344–369. London: Hogarth Press, 1975.

———— (1946). Notes on some schizoid mechanisms. In *The Writings of Melanie Klein*, Vol. 3:1–24. London: Hogarth Press, 1987.

Kohut, H. (1984). *How Does Analysis Cure?* Chicago: University of Chicago Press.

Kris, E. (1938). Laughter as an expressive process: Contributions to the psychoanalysis of expressive behavior. In *Psychoanalytic Explorations in Art*, ed. E. Kris, pp. 217–239. New York: International Universities Press, 1952.

———— (1940). Ego development and the comic. In *Psychoanalytic Explorations in Art*, ed. E. Kris, pp. 204–216. New York: International Universities Press, 1952.

———— (1950). On preconscious mental processes. *Psychoanalytic Quarterly* 19:540–556.

———— (1951). Ego psychology and interpretation in psychoanalytic therapy. *Psychoanalytic Quarterly* 20:15–30.

———— (1952). *Psychoanalytic Explorations in Art*. New York: International Universities Press.

———— (1956a). The recovery of childhood memories in psychoanalysis. *Psychoanalytic Study of the Child* 11:56–78. New York: International Universities Press.

———— (1956b). The personal myth: a problem in psychoanalytic technique. *Journal of the American Psychoanalytic Association* 11:653–658.

Lamm, L. J. (1993). *The Idea of the Past: History, Science and Practice in American Psychoanalysis*. New York and London: New York University Press.

Laquer, T. (1989). *Making Sex: Body and Gender from the Greeks to Freud*. Cambridge, MA: Harvard University Press.

Loewald, H. (1960). On the therapeutic action of psychoanalysis. *International Journal of Psycho-Analysis* 41:16–33.

Loewenstein, R. M. (1956). Some remarks on the role of speech in psychoanalytic technique. *International Journal of Psycho-Analysis* 37:460–468.

Money-Kyrle, R. (1958). The process of psycho-analytical inference. In *The Collected Papers of Roger Money-Kyrle*, ed. D. Meltzer, pp. 343–352. Aberdeen, Scotland: Clinic Press, 1976.

Reich, A. (1951). On counter-transference. *International Journal of Psycho-Analysis* 32:25–31.

——— (1954). Early identifications as archaic elements in the superego. *Journal of the American Psychoanalytic Association* 2:218–238.

Renik, O. (1998). Getting real in psychoanalysis. *Psychoanalytic Quarterly* 67:566–593.

Saks, E. (1999). *Interpreting Interpretation: The Limits of Hermeneutic Psychoanalysis.* New Haven and London: Yale University Press.

Schafer, R. (1968a). *Aspects of Internalization.* New York: International Universities Press.

——— (1968b). The mechanisms of defense. *International Journal of Psycho-Analysis* 49:49–62.

——— (1970). The psychoanalytic vision of reality. *International Journal of Psycho-Analysis* 51:279–297.

——— (1974). Problems in Freud's psychology of women. *Journal of the American Psychoanalytic Association* 22:459–485.

——— (1976). *A New Language for Psychoanalysis.* New Haven: Yale University Press.

——— (1978). *Language and Insight: The Sigmund Freud Memorial Lectures 1975–1976 University College London.* New Haven and London: Yale University Press.

——— (1983). *The Analytic Attitude.* New York: Basic Books.

——— (1988). The sense of an answer: clinical and applied psychoanalysis compared. In *Retelling a Life: Narration and Dialogue in Psychoanalysis,* pp. 165–186. New York: Basic Books.

——— (1992). *Retelling a Life: Narration and Dialogue in Psychoanalysis.* New York: Basic Books.

——— (1994). On gendered discourse and discourse on gender. In *Tradition and Change in Psychoanalysis,* ed. R. Schafer, pp. 35–56. New York: International Universities Press, 1997.

——— (1995). Aloneness in the countertransference. *Psychoanalytic Quarterly* 64:496–516.

——— (1996). Authority, evidence, and knowledge in the psychoanalytic relationship. *Psychoanalytic Quarterly* 65:236–253.

——— (1997a). *Tradition and Change in Psychoanalysis.* New York: International Universities Press.

——— (1997c). *The Contemporary Kleinians of London.* New York: International Universities Press.

——— (2001). Conversations with Elisabeth von R. In *Storms in Her*

*Head: Freud and the Construction of Hysteria*, ed. M. Dimen and A. Harris, pp. 323–340. New York: Other Press.

Segal, H. (1957). Notes on symbol formation. *International Journal of Psycho-Analysis* 38:391–397.

*The Shorter Oxford English Dictionary on Historical Principles*, 2 volumes, revised edition by C. T. Onions, 1973. Oxford: The Clarendon Press.

Spence, D. (1982). *Narrative Truth and Historical Truth: Meaning and Interpretation in Psychoanalysis*. New York: Norton.

Steiner, J. (1993). *Psychic Retreats: Pathological Organizations in Psychotic, Neurotic, and Borderline Patients*. London and New York: Routledge.

Stern, D. B. (1997). *Unformulated Experience: From Dissociation to Imagination*. Hillsdale, NJ: Analytic Press.

Strenger, C. (1991). Between hermeneutics and science: an essay on the epistemology of psychoanalysis. *Psychological Issues 59*. Madison, CT: International Universities Press.

# Index